Cruisin' Through Life At 35MPH

*Six Strategies
to Keep Your
Internal Engine
Running Smoothly*

by Brian Blasko

FINISH LINE PUBLISHING, INC.
Youngstown, Ohio

CONTENTS

gifts. My family, friends, health, education, and the gift of gab are just a few. I love to talk to people. I can talk to anyone at anytime, about anything, in any place. This is my gift and I CHOOSE to use it in a positive way. I have shared conversations with thousands of individuals, while delivering public and private seminars. Heck, I even find that I talk to myself, at least then I know I have a captive listener (well, most of the time). The point is, I haven't let this gift sit on the side of the road, and you shouldn't either. What you don't use, you lose.

The fact that you're reading this book right now means that you are applying your own gifts of sight and reading comprehension. Pat yourselves on the back, you deserve it! You didn't have to purchase this book (unless you're my family), but you chose to. No one forced you to, but *you* took the initiative and I admire that. As you cruise through life, it is easy to forget that YOU need to be the one driving. So often we want to become the passengers and let *others* take responsibility for our successes and failures. Now is the time to take the drivers seat, not tomorrow, not in two hours, but NOW. You have to be the person steering yourself in the right direction, and that can only happen if YOU are the driver!

How many times have you sped through life at 100 mph? I know I have reached that speed many times. Is driving through life too fast a bad thing? Who sets the pace in your life? We as human beings need to find a comfortable speed and then set our cruise control. If we drive over speed bumps and potholes too fast they could cause damage to our vehicles. But what about the personal speed bumps and potholes we encounter everyday? Can they cause some sort of "internal" self-damage? If we fail to see certain road signs while driving, consequences will follow. What about the signs that guide our personal lives? Do we take time to read and understand them?

Every car needs service occasionally. Whether it's an oil change or new spark plugs, maintenance is required. We as humans also need

service. Learning how to give yourself a "tune-up" is very important. If we can keep our internal engines running smoothly, self-maintenance will be minimal. Traffic lights and headlights are necessary while driving a car. If you do not use headlights or yield to traffic lights, you may be putting yourself and others in danger. Every human being has an "inner light." Is yours bright enough to guide you through your highway of life, or does it need recharged? When driving, we usually have a specific destination in mind. Do you have *your* destinations mapped out for your lifetime journey? What are your goals and visions?

The six strategies I share with you as you continue to read, all work. They have been test-driven and proven roadworthy. These strategies are tools for a peaceful journey. Volkswagen has a fantastic slogan that says "On the road of life there are passengers and there are drivers. Drivers Wanted." The same concept applies to you and me. If you are not the one driving yourself through life, then your personal dreams will be minimized and that can lead to a life of potholes, from which you may never escape.

Growing up, many of us had to experience driver education classes. Do you remember yours? Most of us probably sat there daydreaming and thinking, "This is silly, I already know everything I need to know." We sat there for hours and listened about what we should and should not do while driving. We learned stop, go, yield, use the blinkers, never pass on the double yellow lines, etc. We paid our dues, and that was that. Well, my friends, there is no driving school to instruct you on cruisin' through life. It is just you and the open road. *Cruisin' Through Life at 35 MPH* however, is a supplement to that course we never received in driver's education.

My purpose for writing this book is to allow each and every one of you the opportunity to examine your own internal engine. Everyone has gifts to share. I feel it is possible to bring those attributes to the surface through my written experiences offered as learning tools found in the pages of this manuscript. Who knows what contributions they may provide to all humanity as well as to one's self. I simply ask that YOU take the driver's seat and reflect positively on the strategies that follow. Buckle up, start your engines and enjoy the ride!

KNOWING YOUR
SPEED LIMITS

"Patience is the ability to idle your motor, when you feel like stripping your gears"

- Unknown

It was late at night, during the summer of 1996, as I drove through Pennsylvania and received my first, and hopefully last speeding ticket. I remember the day like it was yesterday. I was driving at a speed of 81 mph and to my surprise an unmarked police car was following me. I continued at that speed for two miles before I noticed the red and blue flashing lights in my rear view mirror. My heart sank and I instantly got that "pit" in my stomach, as I'm sure most of you know the feeling. I slowly steered my vehicle over to the right side of the road. Being a public speaker, I thought, no problem, I'm going to talk myself right out of this ticket. I figured if I could motivate thousands of people, I could definitely motivate this officer not to give me a ticket. At my partially wound down window, appeared a face with a mustache and chinstrap, both attached to a rather stately somewhat western-type hat. I could hardly see his face much less talk to it!

"Hello officer," I said in my friendliest voice (you know, the, I'm sorry, please let me off the hook kind of voice). What the heck was I shaking for? What could he do to me if I spoke in my experienced, kinder, softer than normal voice, in my "gift of gab" mode? After all, I'm good at what I do best…talk! I opened my mouth again. All right already, so why wasn't I talking? I actually started to believe the trooper had no intentions of hearing what I had to say. I thought it best to control the words exiting my mouth. My body was shaking and even my thoughts were scared to death.

"Hello young man."

I swallowed hard and took a deep breath. "Did I…did I do something…wrong?" I thought I might as well put on my dumb cap. Attempt the old pretense of innocence bit, the *I didn't know what I was doing* thing.

"I've been following you for approximately two miles. You seem to be in a very big hurry. Did you know that the posted speed limit, and it is posted by the way, is only 50 mph?"

"No, that is, not exactly sir. Ah, how fast, I mean, ah..." he interrupted whatever it was I was trying to say.

"...about 30 more miles per hour, which would explain your inability to see our rather large, painted signs which, by the way, we put up for a reason. May I see your driver's license, please?" He sounded angry, but I had to try again.

"Officer, it's...it's a simple explanation..." I handed him my driver's license.

"Oh I'll bet! Go on, I'm listening. Hope it's original this time. I've heard most all excuses, you know." He shined his small flashlight on my license and began filling in the blanks on his ticket pad as his deep, bass voice seemed to be growling at me. What a time for sudden word loss attack! My mouth moved up and down, but nothing surfaced except babbling idiotic sounds.

"I...ah, ah...sorry...ah, ah...I didn't...ah...mean...sorry...ah, please." Mere jibber-jabber. Well, if there was ever a time I didn't feel exactly like the proud, confident public speaker I was supposed to be, it was then. Great job of defending myself, huh? Where was my gift of gab? After all was said and done, I clutched the $145 ticket in my hand. What a waste of hard earned money. Why was I in such a hurry? I had no business traveling that fast. I learned a valuable lesson that day regarding speed. Don't do it!

I did observe the oversized road sign indicating 50 mph, however, I ignored it completely. No one was around. What the heck! After all, isn't it true that we all take chances now and then? Although one hates to admit to errors as we travel through life, some hasty judgement calls could be very costly.

In life we set many speed limits on our abilities. Sometimes we feel we must speed through at 100 mph and other times we feel like traveling 15 mph. What's a safe speed you might be asking? Only you can be the judge of that. Your pace through life will change, sometimes even from day to day. When you need to be traveling fast, will you be ready? If you need to slow down, will you be able to adjust?

Here is a perfect example. Imagine yourself singing (scary isn't it) in your car, while cruisin' along the highway, at about 75 mph. Everyone around you is traveling the same speed. Traffic seems to be staying together, flowing quickly as one happy family. You look to your left, then right...all of a sudden...BRAKE LIGHTS and SCREECHING TIRES and suddenly everyone slows down to 65 mph. You can only guess what has happened. A police car is out in front of the pack driving at a speed of 68 mph and everyone behind it is traveling at 65 mph! Perhaps troopers or other law enforcement officers enjoy this part of their job most since they can view the entire pack following their pace car through their rear view mirror. Are they possibly thinking "Look at those turkeys behind me. Let me have a little fun with them today." They slowly speed up to 70 mph and what do we do? We speed up to 67 mph. They go 75 mph, we go 72 mph, they slow down to 65 mph and we slow down to 62 mph. In this particular case, the officer on the highway has set the pace.

Now let me ask you this...*who* sets the pace in your life? If you are a parent and you set the pace for your family at 40 mph, chances are they will follow at 37 mph. If you are a manager or supervisor and you arrive at the office cruisin' at 25 mph, your team will follow at 22 mph. If, however, you arrive at 95 mph geared up with a positive attitude, chances are your employees will follow at 92 mph. It is necessary that you set the pace in your life and, at times, help set the pace for others. Who knows, maybe your pace will inspire others.

Remember to always let others know why you have chosen your pace and speed. When others set the pace for us and we become confused, we need to ask why. There is nothing wrong with inquiring why our spouse, partner, client, co-worker, or friend has chosen that pace. If the pace does not feel comfortable, then we must accelerate or brake, whichever the case may warrant. Everyone has the power to influence others in a positive way. Our attitudes and actions make us who we are. I am a firm believer in the quote, "Attitudes are contagious, is *yours* worth catching?" If you have a positive attitude, people will catch it. If you have a negative attitude, people will catch it. The choice is yours!

Let me share a great story about positive and negative attitudes. There was once a psychologist who researched this subject. He placed a child with a negative attitude in a room filled with brand new toys and lots of goodies. There was music, entertainment, candy, you name it, and it was there. He left the child in the room for two hours. The psychologist then took a child with a positive attitude and stuck him in a room filled with horse manure. No games, no toys, just a bunch of manure. This child was also left for two hours. When time was up, the psychologist entered the room where the negative child had been with the new toys. He found the child throwing a temper tantrum. "How dare you stick me in this room with all of this stuff and only give me two hours to play?" The child was still negative. He then checked on the positive boy in the room with the horse manure. He was shocked beyond belief with his discovery. You see, as he entered the room he saw the child diving and swimming in the horse manure. He could not believe his eyes. "What are you doing?" the researcher asked. The child looked up excitedly and exclaimed, "You can't fool me, with all this horse manure there's gotta be a pony around here somewhere!" Great story, right? Yes it is. Sometimes in life we may feel like we are stuck in horse manure, but always remember, at least we still have air-freshener. Your attitude and how you view things make all the difference in the world.

When we speed in our cars we are taking chances and risking tickets, our lives, and the lives of others. So why do we do it? Why *do* we sometimes go against our better judgement and speed through our personal lives? There are no police officers available to give us tickets as we fumble or speed through life. Only YOU know the proper pace and right speed with which to travel through your daily routine. If you travel too fast or too slow, you may miss out on some of the finer things life has to offer. How do we find a comfortable speed? The answer is quite simple. Take a few "test" drives to find your comfort zone. If a current situation in your life is bogging you down, acceleration might be the right choice. On the other hand, if your life seems to be moving at a super fast pace, applying the brakes might be a good decision. Sometimes we must accelerate the pace and at other times, we need to sit back and enjoy the scenery. Only you can decide which to do and when. If you make a wrong decision, learn from it. Always remember to stop, look, and listen before shifting gears!

If you are a passenger in a car and the driver is speeding, then you are at risk and have no control. If you become a passenger in *life*, you will have less control over choices being made because *other* forces will be driving you. When you take control of your life and speed limits, your roads will be paved with opportunity.

Throughout my career as a speaker, I have had the privilege to meet many wonderful individuals. During my encounters with these individuals, I've conducted an extensive amount of research. For two years, I asked participants in my seminars one simple question. "If the posted speed limit on a major highway was 65 mph how many of you would be going over the speed limit?" The results will surprise you. 97 percent answered yes! The second question was, "What could happen if you were caught?" The number one response was, "Get a ticket." There were many snickers and no one seemed to take this question seriously. I then addressed the listeners with the matter of taking chances in life. "If you are willing to take risks on the road, why wouldn't you take even more risks in your personal life?" Silence prevailed.

It is true that each of us take many unnecessary risks while driving, but when it comes to our personal lives we tend to hit the brakes. Nothing comes easy. Risk taking is an essential part of life. Be aware of the risks you take, think them through and then proceed accordingly. If you always do what you always did, you will always get what you always got. A most famous gentleman was once asked how he became so successful. His response was simply, "I failed my way to the top!" That man was Thomas Edison.

We live in a society that enjoys instant gratification. Gimme, gimme, gimme! Now, now, now! We want things quick and we want them easy. Why do you think the microwave was invented? We have instant coffee, instant mashed potatoes, instant oil changes, instant money access, minute rice, fast food, and the list goes on and on. However, some of the greatest accomplishments that we have already seen, took years to achieve. For example, quality education, engines with more horse-power, computers, the Internet, and The Ohio State Buckeyes beating the Michigan Wolverines, just to name a few. We want everything in life and we want it NOW! I admit, I've been guilty of thinking this way many times. When I graduated from college, I wanted to be instantaneously rich. I've been finished now for many years and I still haven't been asked to be on the cover of *Forbes* magazine. What does that tell me? It tells me that I wanted too much too soon and my goal was unrealistic.

Sometimes the reason we fail to reach our goals is because we set them so high that not even the highest flying bird could reach them. When we do not achieve the goals we've set for ourselves, we feel inadequate. Therefore, we must set our personal speed limits on a reasonable cruise control in order to achieve our goals. Begin small and gradually grow larger. In fact, for each goal set, we need to remember that sub-goals are required. For example, if I want to get the Anderson account in two months, and I make an effort to achieve this feat without proper planning, I may have problems. When we set big hairy, scary goals for ourselves, we often forget that there are little "pit stops" that need to be taken along the way. To land the Anderson account, I will spend the first week researching the client. The second week I will meet with my em-ployer, and during the third week I will staff people to assist me. After I have finished my last sub-goal, the project, or large goal, will definitely be accomplished. (More details about goal setting at Mile Marker #6.)

As I mentioned earlier, YOU need to be the one driving yourself through life at a reasonable speed, if you want to succeed. There are many negative forces in life that can take the form of "driver," such as, drugs, alcohol, other people, bad attitudes, and fear. Many times it is easier to let these things take the driver's seat for us, but remember, when we are not driving, we do not have control. Let me share with you a story about an old college buddy of mine who rode shotgun for a long, long time. We'll call this man "Pete the Passenger." Pete always liked to cruise through life at about 150 mph. He took many short cuts through life, some led to success, while others led him down roads of hardship. Pete had no control over his destinations because his drivers were drugs and alcohol. He was merely a "passenger" on a road leading nowhere and the drugs were driving him out of control. One day Pete finally slowed down his lifestyle, but it wasn't by choice, his drivers drove him right into a temporary pit stop… jail. Could this penal time spent behind bars calm him down and make him realize that HE needed to take the driver's seat? Could Pete take the steering wheel of life once again? Family and friends could help "set the pace" for a peaceful recovery, but only Pete could take the driver's seat.

Once out of jail however, he became a passenger again, prefer-ring to cruise through life fast and easy. He wanted everything and he wanted it <u>now</u>. Pete was continuously putting himself and his loved ones in jeopardy. When we lose control of our actions, we lose control of the steering wheel and our personal driving abilities. Pete became a passen-ger on a journey in which he had little control, or did he?

It's all in how we "act" (not react) to our situation that makes the difference. Pete was forced to "react" to circumstances in life because he chose to ride shotgun. However, the day *he* decided to take the driver's seat was the day *he* began to act. There are many obstacles in the road. In this particular case, Pete's obstacles, drugs and alcohol, were control-lable. He realized he could determine his destinations by taking over the driver's seat. He just needed to <u>act</u> on it. Before long, drugs and alcohol began to take a "back seat" in Pete's life. His inner light was alive once again! His daily actions became a reflection of his positive attitude. He started treating himself with more respect and with that, came fulfill-ment.

Pete's situation taught him that being the driver is a much more productive way to cruise through life. If Pete can do it why can't others? Guess what…they can! How many of you have a "Pete the Passenger" in your own lives? If you know of someone who is the passenger on a road leading to nowhere, sit them down and talk about what you see. Your caring attitude and support could be the best pit stop he/she may ever have. Although they may have put up their tinted windows and become blind to their actions, it does not mean you can't roll them down again. YOU may need to be one of the drivers that can help influence them in a powerful, positive way. Become a back seat driver to a friend!

I am a firm believer that we have the power to change and influ-ence others. This issue has been argued by many. Some of my colleagues, excellent speakers, believe that you can not change anyone…*unless* they want to be changed. Personally, I disagree with this statement. I believe we *can* change people without them even wanting it to happen. I do agree that their change does have to come from within, but I believe we can influence that change without them even realizing it.

Let me give you an example to think about. Have you ever been in a bad mood? If you're like most people, and I'm talking about the other six billion people in the world, you probably just said yes. Now, have you ever been in a bad mood because work got on your nerves? If you said yes continue reading, if you said no, then please let me know where you work because I would like to send my resume. There may have been times when you left work saying, "I dislike every customer, client and co-worker in my organization and I never want to go to work again!" Then to make things worse, on the drive home, someone cuts you off. Now you're really upset. In fact, you decide to pull up beside that person and tell them you think they're number #1. But you don't use your "pointer" finger to tell them ☺

You finally reach home, and are about to walk through the front door, where you'll be greeted by your spouse, partner, boyfriend, girlfriend, cousin, friend, lover, child, dog, or cat. Now remember, you are angry and upset, but as soon as you open that front door, they immediately jump into your arms and start licking your face……the dog or cat I'm talking about (maybe your spouse greets you like that who knows), but has that special person ever said, mommy, daddy, honey, brother, sister, sweetheart, I Love You! They give you a great big hug and all of a sudden…POOF. You are not angry anymore. Has something like that ever happened to you? You're darn right it has. Guess what? THEY CHANGED YOU! Maybe it was their love, their smile, or their lick of the face. Whatever they did, it changed your attitude. How do I know *they* changed *you?* I know in my heart you did not leave work in a bad mood thinking, "I'm MAD, but, I'm going to let someone change me when I get home." It was probably the furthest thought from your mind. It just happened!

There are some people, for whatever reason, who will not allow their attitudes to be influenced and will do everything in their power to remain miserable. These folks, nevertheless, require your love and effort. Studies have shown that about one percent of the world's population will not like you. When I first heard this statistic I thought "No big deal," until I did the math. There are currently about six billion people, give or take a million, living in this world, which means one percent represents about 60 million people. Wow! You will never meet all of these individuals, but sometimes when I'm on the road speaking, I feel like I have all one percent right there in the room with me. Remember this, you can not always make people happy, but darn it, you can sure try.

Changing our own personal mindset and behavior has to do with something called the "self-fulfilling prophecy." According to communication scholars Insel, Jaccobson, & Merton, "A self-fulfilling prophecy occurs when you make a prediction or formulate a belief that comes true *because* you made the prediction and acted on it as if it were true." It means self-talk or intra-personal communication. In simpler terms, communication with one's own self. Self-talk can be positive or negative, it's up to you. If you tell yourself you're going to win a race, your odds of winning increase. On the other hand, if you tell yourself you're going to lose, chances are you will. How does this relate to us? When we tell ourselves that our day is lousy and we are unhappy, it becomes our reality. However, when you tell yourself that your day is going well and that you *are* happy, chances are your day will go well and you *will* become happier. Believing in your positive self-talk is key. Have you been finding the "positives" in your life, or have you been looking for the negatives? Both are just around the corner, it's up to you to decide which one to choose.

Let's talk for a moment about procrastination. Nah, we'll get to that later. You see, I just did it. I want to ask you one question and I want an honest answer. Do *you*…procrastinate? Come on, some of you are doing it right *now* just in giving me an answer. It is a hard question to answer, but the majority of us, including myself, would have to say yes. Have you ever met someone who was so bad they told you they were going to procrastinate later? What a play on words! The best way to help eliminate the "P" word is to take one step at a time. When we say we are going to clean our entire house, it seems like such a big task, that we may tend to "put it off," because we do not have time to actually clean the *whole* house. If however, you say you'll clean one room at a time you're more likely to clean it because the task will not seem so overwhelming. Speaking of procrastination, I wanted to have this book written seven years ago…just kidding.

Another way to stop procrastination is to tell other people what it is you have been procrastinating about. Not only does it hold you accountable, it offers you a support team. If you want to quit smoking and you tell 30 people that you want this to happen within six months, during that six-month period you have 30 people nagging, bugging, and bumming smokes from you. You are no longer alone. By the same token, if you fail to quit smoking within that six-month time frame, you may feel like you have let 30 people down. Other people can definitely help stop procrastination.

Let me share with you one way I was helped regarding the completion of this book. A few years ago I conducted a workshop for a youth leadership class in Knox County, Indiana. The program and the individuals involved were wonderful and I had a blast. I became friends with all of the students and remained in contact with many of them after the two-day workshop ended. However, one particular student, Kelly, corresponded through weekly e-mail. One day while typing her a message, I mentioned that it would be cool if every time she e-mailed me, she would include the word BOOK somewhere in the context to remind me of my goal. Did she do it? You bet. Did it help? You bet. To return the favor, I started to include certain words in my e-mail that would remind her of the things *she* had been procrastinating about. This method of support really helped and I appreciated and looked forward to receiving her e-mail. Thanks Kelly! Remember, it's easier cruisin' with others when they're on the same road as you.

Let's relive our youth for a moment. I want to reminisce with you about your **first** driving experience. I'm referring to when you were two years old. That's right, we cruised through life at age two, but hopefully someone else was steering. I'm talking about your first red wagon here folks! Do you remember being pulled around the yard? It was great. We just sat back and enjoyed the ride. We had no worries. We did not have to think about steering or what speed we were traveling. Life was good. Someone *else* took control for us.

As we got a little older, we received our first big wheel or tricycle. At this stage in life *we* wanted more control. Being the one steering and peddling was neat! Now we actually had choices regarding our destinations. Even though our destinations were limited to the driveway, we were in the driver's seat and that's all that mattered. Speaking of the driver's seat. My dad used to let me sit on his lap and steer his car when I was younger. I used to think it was the greatest thing ever. I remember going to school the next day and telling my friends that I got to drive his car all by myself. When in actuality, I only got to steer and my dad's hands were still on the wheel (but my friends didn't need to know that information).

Next we moved on to the bicycle with training wheels. We were so proud of ourselves. At this stage we still had control over cruisin' around the driveway and maybe even ventured out into the street with parental supervision. We were on top of the world and it was hard to fall off because of those nifty training wheels. We peddled up and down, up and down, up and down, and up and down that driveway of ours over and over and over again. Life was great!

Eventually, the big day arrived. Time to take off the training wheels. How did you feel? Probably a little excited and nervous at the same time. We thought, "Yeah, I'm a big person now!" But at this stage in life most of us had to resort *back* to getting help from someone else. Although we were growing up fast, we still needed to have that person running along side of us each step of the way. Then one magical morning it happened. The person who had been running along side you finally decided it was time to let go. Off you went, SLAM, face first into the pavement! Most of us either cried or were shocked beyond crying. We were *so* big, but we still needed help. Back to supervision and someone running beside the bike. After what seemed like running the distance of a marathon, the person guiding you once again let go. This time, you made it five feet before falling. The next attempt you made it 15 feet, then 50 feet, then 100 feet until before you knew it, you were finally riding by yourself. What a feeling of accomplishment! You were in TOTAL control. But bruises, scrapes, cuts, and maybe even broken bones were some of the consequences of cruisin' on your own.

After riding the bicycle for what seemed like a thousand years, some of us moved up another stage. The go-kart, mo-ped, or dirt bike made their debut appearance. Now we became drivers with *speed* and life was really looking good. You were the envy of all the neighborhood kids. In fact, the summer you got your motorized vehicle, you suddenly had more friends. You rode around the neighborhood or in the woods at every chance. Riding was fun but you *still* had limits.

Eventually, you became bored and began setting your sights even higher. Your SIXTEENTH birthday! Driving the little motorized vehicle was nice, but a car, now that was a different story all together. Try to remember the feelings you had when you first received your driver's license. Yep, that's right aaaaaaaaalllllllll those years ago. How did you feel? If you were like most people you probably felt pride, excitement, nervousness, and responsibility all wrapped into one. The self-satisfaction was amazing. You couldn't wait to pick up your friends and hit the town. In fact, you probably looked forward to *always* driving everywhere. Driving was cool! We were the rulers of our fate and the masters of our destiny!

When we were younger, all we ever wanted to do was drive, drive, drive. Well, now that we're older do we still feel the same way? Chances are, no. Why? Driving in today's world has become not only routine and monotonous but frightening as well. It has lost its excitement and the "fun" we used to have. Driving in traffic today is sometimes a big pain in the "ass"elerator! Many of us have become simply tired of driving because gas is too expensive and maintenance costs are high. We either need new tires, brakes, radiators, or oil changes. Not to mention it's your turn in the car pool. It seems society is traveling in one speed, super-sonic.

As we grow older, life is pretty much the same way. Things become more complicated and stressful. My advice is to push your pedal to the metal and go have some fun today. Do something different, something you would have done if you were 16 all over again (let's keep it legal this time). As we advance in age, we could begin to lose our creative juices and become stuck in ruts. Get off the side of the road and generate some excitement. Make a funny face at the child in the car next to you. Sing and dance in your car without worrying about what others may think. When life becomes mundane, do something about it! Look up a new word in the dictionary and use it today. Laugh at yourself more. Smile more. Hug more. Kiss more. Love more. Be more thankful. Live today as if it were your first, last, and only day on earth. Let's face it, a lot of you reading right now aren't 16 anymore, but that doesn't mean you can't act like it every once in awhile.

Our various driving stages in life have and always will be embedded into our memories. The stages were set up to ensure a safe journey while we cruised through life from childhood through adolescence to adulthood. From our first little red wagon, to our brand new shiny car, we continually progressed forward. In what stage are *you* currently driving? Are you out on your own, or have you reverted back to the days of youth, still letting *others* take control for you? Never be afraid to let others help you through your various stages in life, but eventually, you have to be the one who takes over the steering wheel.

This first Mile Marker was designed to make you aware of your cruisin' speeds in life. We need to be the one setting the pace, stopping procrastination, thinking positive, and overcoming hurry sickness. When we have a grasp on our various speeds in life, happiness is just around the corner. Remember that you can not do everything all the time, but you can most definitely enjoy the things you are doing now. If you're unhappy with your current speed of life, change it!

CRUISIN' CONCEPTS TO CONSIDER...

• *Set the pace*

• *Stop procrastinating*

• *Think positive*

• *Take the driver's seat NOW*

• *Know your speed limits*

SPEED BUMPS AND POTHOLES

"If the road to success is not smooth, switch lanes."

- Brian Blasko

I'm sure most of you would agree that speed bumps are a good thing, but at the same time, a pain in the rump. Am I right or wrong? Speed bumps seem to aggravate us most when we are in a hurry, rushing from here to there. They are carefully placed in spaced intervals to warn those drivers who are traveling at a rapid, unsafe speed. Speed bumps remind us to slow down and take caution. What about life's speed bumps? Are they also there for us, serving the same purpose? We used the example of Pete in Mile Marker #1. If he had been more careful, perhaps he could have guided himself over certain speed bumps, had he taken the driver's seat earlier in life.

Cement mounds on the road or in a parking lot serve a purpose and, although many are annoyed by their presence, they do assure our safety. They are reminders of what *not* to do, speed. We need these "reminders" as we cruise through our daily lives because they keep us aware of what is good, bad, right, or wrong.

Two of the greatest speed bumps I know are my mom and dad. That's right, our parents, family, and friends are considered speed bumps throughout our entire lives. At a very early age, our parents or guardians instruct us regarding most of the bends along the road, including many turns towards the good, bad, rights, and wrongs. They actually provide those "safety bumps" we encounter in life for the sole purpose of protecting our well being. They assist us as we approach each one. Growing up with two wonderful parents made my early journey through life very smooth.

Of course, as I grew older, I managed to hit several speed bumps on my own. Sure, I made some poor decisions, but at least I had the opportunity to experience them as my own driver. We can only learn from our mistakes. Some parents place their children upon pedestals, forbidding them from constructing and enacting their own decisions. This is not a healthy path for any child to take. Of course parents should protect, guide, and steer their children towards the right direction, but they should also know at what stage to let go. In fact, as a parent, one of the primary responsibilities *is* to guide your children in the right direction. My question is, what happens the day mom and dad have no choice but to cease driving? Will their children be ready for that sudden, drastic change? Will they possess the ability to follow their *own* correct course? Only time will tell.

If you have ever traveled through Ohio, or live in Ohio like I do, then you already know about potholes. I have encountered many, many, many, many, many, many, many, many, many (you get the point) potholes while driving. Some potholes have even been known to swallow up small children whole! It seems as if we get snow about 12 months a year, so, potholes are an inevitable feature in the road. A few winters ago I rescued my wife, Laura, from a pothole related flat tire. Her car had hit a huge, unavoidable hole and as a result, she was rewarded with a flat tire. She immediately called me from her car phone and explained the situation. Within minutes I arrived on the scene with a flashlight and tire iron in hand. I changed the flat and all was well. My wife was in a pinch and I helped her out. Her vehicular damage was repairable. But what about the potholes we hit on our personal journeys through life? Is the damage just as repairable?

Getting over or around each pothole will not be the easiest or simplest thing to do. What will come in handy to assist you will be that strong positive outlook which we previously mentioned. Having an optimistic outlook on life is a great place to begin. If you are breathing right now (check your pulse) then you should be smiling for the simple breaths you take. Having high self-esteem will help you get over the many potholes that complicate your daily life.

SOME COMMON EVERYDAY POTHOLES MAY INCLUDE:

- Depression

- Illness

- Financial difficulty

- Disagreements

- Rejection

- Job stress

- Unemployment

- Divorce

- Failure

- Loneliness

- Headaches

- Toothaches

- Rainy days

- Cold days

- Hot days

- Death of a loved one

- And the list continues….

- _____   _____   _____

If, after reading this list you can think of any other potholes within your daily life, please write them down. Just keep in mind that every pothole cannot be avoided, but something *can* be done to help patch each one. You need to focus on what is the most important hole to be repaired and deal with it first. All of your daily potholes can be patched up, but YOU are going to need some equipment such as, dedication, motivation, high self-esteem, and a most definite positive attitude! You cannot always wait for someone else to come along and fix things. Sometimes, you are stuck with your own repair project. Just like the actual potholes in the road, the damage may not be corrected for six months or more. If you travel to work everyday utilizing the same road, and encounter major potholes, what do you do? Take an alternate route. Certainly there is more than one way to get to your destination. This same concept of finding an alternate route applies to life.

Some of life's potholes are big, some are small and some we blow out of proportion. Our bigger potholes, such as the death of a loved one or divorce, are naturally tougher to fill. Maybe, we should stop trying to fill them all at once. Take baby steps and patch up your problems a little at a time, something like road crews patching up sections of the road. Did you ever notice, for time and budget purposes, before re-paving an entire street, the road crew will fill each individual pothole over and over until the hole has reached an extraordinarily dangerous depth and repair is no longer feasible. Only then, will they tear up the road and re-pave the entire thing making the path perfectly smooth, enabling travel to continue. If they can do it to our roads, then why can't we fill our personal potholes slowly the same way? We can! When tragedy occurs, begin the healing process with one shovel of "gravel patch" at a time.

About four years ago a friend of mine went through a rather unpleasant divorce. There are a number of different reasons why divorce is difficult. A feeling of failure ranks at the top. *Not* failure because you and your spouse could not get along, but instead, the self-deterioration you feel because you could not make it *work*.

This couple had been married for approximately four years before things began to sour. Many people thought all would blow over. On the surface both held professional positions, had money and a lovely home. They showed their love in public, everything seemed so fairy-tale right. However, the husband confided in me that the divorce proceedings were creating some mild depression. This was becoming a roadblock for him. I made many attempts to help him adjust and partially fill this large pothole. His family and friends were continuously comforting him as well. When he was feeling down in the dumps, we were his **support team.** Did all of our efforts take the pain away? Of course not, but our support did assist him in his recovery process. We did not pave the entire road but instead, helped by shoveling gravel patch every chance we got. The couple has gone their separate ways and are doing well while still remaining friends. Their new journeys through life have begun. How many of you know of a similar situation? Have you had the opportunity to be someone *else's* gravel patch lately? Thanks Deric, for showing me a fine example of perseverance!

There's a Hole in My Sidewalk written by Portia Nelson
I
I walk down the street.
There is a deep hole in the sidewalk.
I fall in.
I am lost...I am helpless.
It wasn't my fault.
It takes forever to find a way out.

II

I walk down the same street.
There is a deep hole in the sidewalk.
I pretend I don't see it.
I fall in again.
I can't believe I am in the same place.
But, it isn't my fault.
It still takes a long time to get out.

III

I walk down the same street.
There is a deep hole in the sidewalk.
I see it is there.
I still fall in. It's a habit.
My eyes are open.
I know where I am.
It's my fault. I get out immediately.

IV

I walk down the same street.
There is a deep hole in the sidewalk.
I walk around it.

V

I walk down another street.

Let's talk a moment about self-esteem. *Webster's* defines esteem as to regard favorably; respect. Having high self-esteem means you respect yourself and regard yourself favorably. Low self-esteem means you look unfavorably upon yourself and lack self-respect. Between you and me, I'll take high self-esteem every time! Now, I realize we are not always going to be happy, happy, joy, joy. It is quite natural to get down on ourselves and become depressed. At the same time, it is easy to gain our esteem back. There are many different things we can do to build higher self-esteem. One suggestion I can offer is to find one particular thing within your life, which you do with much expertise. Then simply make it very clear to your own self that you are indeed, the best at what you do. Be realistic. For example, I like basketball, but I know I am not better then Michael Jordan. But maybe I can be the best in the state of Ohio, or in my city, or in my school, or in my neighborhood, or on my street, or even in my house. Find that something which may range from cooking to singing to typing to writing to playing cards. I guarantee you are great at something. Find that something and enjoy it!

Another way to build higher self-esteem almost instantly is doing something nice for someone else. Have you ever noticed when you do something kind for others, you actually feel good about yourself? It's one of the neatest feelings in the world. Chances are, you have helped someone in the past who didn't even ask for it, and you felt great. My dad, Steve, is famous for this. Let me share with you a story about Steve, the beach, and a man named Randy.

When I was younger my family and I would often take trips to the beach. Each summer we would load up the old family station wagon and head to Ocean City, Maryland for a week of fun in the sun. We played in the ocean all day and walked the beaches and boardwalk all night. During our evening strolls along the beach we viewed unique sand sculptures left untouched. Many resembled ancient museum pieces, while others were more comical in their appearance. Some were nice, some were great, but each night, we would see one in particular that stood above the rest in its beauty and design. These sculptures we admired most were of religious scenes. Every night a man would make his way down to the beach just before sunset to start his masterpiece. We did not know the man's name because we actually never saw him perform his work, but soon, that all changed.

One evening, my dad decided to venture down the boardwalk a bit earlier so that he could watch this artist perform his magic. He stood in amazement as the man carved wet sand with a small knife and then carefully patted each section into place. Each effort resulted in a magnificent sculpture. During one of my father's earlier visits, he had the chance to speak with the man we now call, Randy. They spoke for quite some time on a few different occasions. During their conversations, my dad discovered that Randy was remodeling his home and was in the process of hanging dry wall. (I don't know if you've ever hung dry wall, but it is not a fun job.) Randy explained that he was having a hard time finishing the job because he was working alone. My father, being the kind spirited man he is, did what he does best, he offered to help.

When my family learned what my father was about to do for a stranger he just met, let alone while being on this supposedly relaxing vacation, we were astonished. The next morning he woke up at 5 a.m., not to exercise, see the sunrise, or walk on the beach. No. Instead, he woke up to hang dry wall. He was up and out the door before any of us even had a chance to hit the snooze button once. About 10 a.m. dad returned from Randy's house and spent the rest of the day with the family. He could not stop talking about how beautiful this man's house was. Well, it was fabulous, and how do I know, because the next morning I woke up at 5 a.m. to help hang dry wall! I spent four hours at a stranger's house that morning and it was at that moment in my life, I realized my dad was truly one of my greatest influences. I learned from him, through not only his words, but his *actions* as well. He spent two mornings of his vacation helping a complete stranger fix his home. Those two days were no sweat off his back, but the impact they must have made on Randy will probably last a lifetime.

I was taught a valuable lesson that vacation I will never forget. Time spent helping others, is time well spent. We went on that vacation to receive some much-deserved relaxation. What we left with however, was better then any day at the beach. Randy had a little pothole and we made sure he had help filling it one shovel of gravel patch at a time. Thanks dad for showing me the *true meaning* of a random act of kindness. When you find someone like Randy who needs help, don't turn your head in another direction as you might miss out on the opportunity of a lifetime. It's not every day we get a chance to do the "right thing." When your day comes, seize the moment.

In our daily lives, there will always be a pothole or two. Whether it's money problems, aches and pains, unexpected car repairs, or a much larger gas or electric bill, obstacles exist. How can we get over them? How do we make our obstacles disappear? It's simple, do not avoid them. It is a known fact most of us probably spend more time whining about our potholes instead of paving them. Life is too short to be lived in this manner. When you are faced with a pothole, deal with it. I know it is easier to run from our problems, but eventually they will catch up with us. When they finally do catch up, they are usually bigger than when they first appeared.

As a public speaker, I continuously have the opportunity to meet many types of individuals working in different environments. Some have visible potholes while others keep theirs well concealed. A few years ago, while delivering one of my public communication seminars, I met two amazing individuals. One of the individuals was blind and the other was confined to a wheel chair, paralyzed from the waist down. Now remember, I was delivering an interpersonal communication seminar. When I first saw these two individuals arrive, I thought to myself, "Wow, what courage it must have taken for them to be here." I quickly realized that I would have to accommodate them so they did not feel uncomfortable.

During the past few years, I held that particular seminar over 150 times. Some statistics and material naturally came out the same almost every seminar I delivered. When it was time for me to discuss "eye focus," I said, "It is imperative to look into someones eyes while communicating, otherwise they may not feel comfortable." At that same moment, my eyes met those of the blind man. I'm sure you can imagine how I felt. How could I let that comment slip out of my mouth when sitting in front of me, no more then 10 feet away, was this courageous man?

Almost instantaneously I came up with a happier tone to my speech. "A smile is 10 times better than any eye focus, but the smile of a man who cannot see is 1,000 times better!" Jerry smiled and others laughed. Had I redeemed myself? I had no clue until the first break arrived. I made a point to walk over and speak with Jerry. I'll admit, at first I was nervous. I thought he might be angry with me for trying to cover up my comment. Then Jerry said something I will never forget. "Brian, shut your eyes for moment and enter my world." After being stunned for a few seconds, I quickly complied, keeping my eyes shut for the entire five-minute conversation. He told me, "Brian, you are one of the best speakers I have ever heard." Then he said jokingly, "You would probably be the best speaker I have ever seen, had I not been lacking in that department." He took no offense and asked me to keep up the good work. Jerry taught me a lesson that day. Use what you have to the best of your abilities and don't sweat what you don't have. He may have had no eye focus that day, but his zest for life was more refreshing than any eye focus I had ever seen.

Lets talk about "gas" for a moment, and I don't mean the kind that makes people clear the room after you've eaten a plate of beans. I'm talking about the kind that makes your car move. Let me share something called "The Full-Tank Factor." For years, I have been comparing my self-esteem levels to an automobile's gas gauge. Let me explain. When you are driving your car with a full tank of gas, how do you feel? Do you have that "sky's the limit" feeling? Certainly, because you are ready to go anywhere and you feel **secure** and **confident** of a safe arrival. When the gas gauge reads three-quarters full, you still have that good, secure feeling. Even at half a tank you're probably comfortable. However, once you go below that half-tank level, something happens. In your mind, you start to subconsciously think about stopping to purchase fuel. You can still travel, but knowing you should get gasoline soon, begins to cause worry. How far is the nearest gas station? Your gauge now reads one-quarter of a tank, meaning this is it. You can't let your tank go down any lower. But still, you don't quite have time to stop. Instead you keep putting it off, and putting it off, and putting it off, until the day comes when you hear ding, ding, ding and look down to see the gas light is on. Why do most of us wait until the last minute to refuel anyway? Finally, when your car is running on nothing but fumes, you make it to the gas station. When you purchase the petrol, you feel refreshed once again!

I believe the same concept applies to our self-esteem. When life is going well for us, we are confident and happy, with self-esteem at a high peak. Perhaps we need a new philosophy in life…I'VE GOT GAS. Sounds like a great slogan to me. How do we want to use this phrase? The bottom line is, we need to do things that provide us with enough GAS (esteem) to continue through life. What could you do? There are many ways to provide your human engine with GAS. Compliment or help someone, read a good book, sing in the shower, go dancing, spend time with loved ones, find your own Pete, Deric, or Randy and talk with them. When we accomplish things we are proud of, we *gain* GAS. When we do things we are ashamed of, we begin to *lose* GAS. If our internal tank levels are always reading three-quarters or fuller, then, as we go up against the low periods in our lives, we will not run out. However, if we are living our lives below half a tank, life will seem to be abusing us and we'll have no GAS to feel good about ourselves.

If you are working on a major project at work and feeling quite overwhelmed, having GAS will help you. Even if you do something small for your company, do it well and you will supply GAS for your personal tank. **Creating happiness in your professional and personal life is up to you.** Having GAS can help you fulfill that happiness. High self-esteem takes daily time and energy and requires more work than one realizes. Can we naturally have high self-esteem? Yes, but even those individuals who always seem to have a full tank, still need to hit the station once in awhile. When was the last time *you* had a personal fill-up?

Extensive amounts of research have gone into the topic of self-esteem. One of the greatest stories I have heard regarding this topic comes from an audio tape set created by Jack Canfield, one of the co-authors of the *Chicken Soup for the Soul* book series. In his tape series *How to Build High Self-Esteem,* Jack tells the story of a little boy playing baseball. One day this youngster goes outside with a baseball bat and ball and stands in the middle of the yard. He decides he is going to play by himself, throwing the ball into the air and swinging at it while it falls to the ground. Before he tosses the ball into the air, the boy says to himself, "I am the world's greatest baseball player." He throws, swings, and misses the ball completely. He quickly picks up the ball and says again, "I am the world's greatest baseball player." Again, he swings and misses. He repeats this process one more time with the same results. Then suddenly a little light goes off inside his head and he says with confidence, "I am the greatest *pitcher* that ever lived!" The moral of the story…focus positively on your strengths whatever they may be. When we focus **positively**, we gain higher self-esteem.

Have you ever ridden over a "rumble strip?" You know, the things that go brubrubrurbru and vibrate your body and car as you ride over them. I am thankful for the person who put those rumble strips on the road. Most toll booth plazas on the turnpike have rumble strips set up about 100 yards before you reach the booths. You're driving along, when all of the sudden you hear and feel brubrubrubru, then you travel another 20 yards and again you feel brubrubrubru until you finally reach the booth. Rumble strips serve almost the same purpose as speed bumps. They are there to slow you down and keep you alert.

About two years ago, I was pulled over on the Ohio turnpike. This time I wasn't speeding. Honest! This time, I was sleeping. Let me explain. When I was in graduate school I lived in Cleveland, Ohio for about two years. My family and friends lived in Youngstown, Ohio. Since I lived away from home, I would often commute back and forth so I could visit friends and family. The distance between Cleveland and Youngstown is 75 miles. One evening, while driving back to Cleveland, I was having a hard time staying awake. I would close my eyes for what seemed like an hour, but in actuality, it was only a few seconds. I would find myself waking up in the next lane. If you have ever experienced this, you could imagine my fright. This went on for about 30 minutes or so. Every once in a while I would find myself hitting the mini rumble strips placed along the side of the road, which woke me up immediately. After sporadically switching lanes and hitting rumble strips for a number of miles I finally saw the red and blue flashing lights in my rear view mirror. I once again got that instant pit in the stomach feeling. "Oh boy," I thought, "What have I done now?" I quickly pulled the car to the side of the road and got out my license and registration. I dreaded the thought of getting a ticket because money was tight and I did not want my insurance to go up again. The officer approached.

"Son, have you been drinking?"

"No Sir. I've been sleeping!" The look on his face was priceless.

"What did you say?"

"I said, I've been sleeping, officer."

"No drinking though, huh?"

"No Sir, just coffee in my thermos. I was in Youngstown visiting my family and I'm trying to get back home."

"I smell the coffee. Better drink some more. Might keep you awake. Follow me to the nearest rest stop, please. It's only a few miles up the road. You can rest there." When we arrived at the rest area, he let me off the hook with just a warning. He made me promise to rest a little before I got back on the road. I ended up sleeping for about 45 minutes. I woke up refreshed and made it back to Cleveland safely. That officer was a major rumble strip for me that night. If he hadn't stopped me, who knows what might have happened. He helped me when I needed it and I am thankful. When was the last time you were a rumble strip for yourself or someone you know?

This second Mile Marker was designed to enable you to realize that, although we may confront potholes daily, it doesn't mean we have to stay in them. The speed bumps we hit on the road also serve a purpose. We need to be more aware and cautious of our personal speed bumps. Life is a journey that should be fun. When you hit a speed bump in life, use it to grow personally. When you encounter a pothole, begin filling it with one shovel of gravel patch at a time.

Here is a sketch of Abraham Lincoln's road to the White House
Talk about speed bumps and potholes…He definitely had a few!

1831- Failed in Business

1832- Defeated for Legislature

1833- Second Failure in Business

1836- Suffered Nervous Breakdown

1838- Defeated for Speaker

1840- Defeated for Elector

1843- Defeated for Congress

1848- Defeated for Congress

1855- Defeated for Senate

1856- Defeated for Vice President

1858- Defeated for Senate

1860- **ELECTED PRESIDENT!**

CRUISIN' CONCEPTS TO CONSIDER...

- *Learn from life's little speed bumps*

- *Begin paving your potholes one shovel of gravel patch at a time*

- *Keep your self-esteem level (gas tank) full*

- *I'VE GOT GAS*

- *Random acts of kindness are cool*

READING THE
ROAD SIGNS

"The only limit to our realization of tomorrow will be our doubts of today."

- Franklin Delano Roosevelt

As we continue to travel the various roadways of life, we will observe many different signs along the way. These signs keep our mind in a fresh state by guiding, instructing, and reminding us what we must do next. They range from speed limits to stop, go, yield the right of way, slow down, sharp turn, curve ahead, slippery when wet, railroad crossing, and the list goes on. They have each been placed within vision above, below, or directly in front of all drivers. Their placement has been carefully designed and cannot be missed unless, of course, the driver is sleeping.

I can describe in one word what would happen if we did not have road signs…Chaos! If there were no signs, there would be no direction. You would still be able to manage your driving, but I guarantee, it would be confusing. Keep in mind that even though you think you know each sign by heart, signs can change at the snap of a finger.

Throughout this Mile Marker we will examine many personal road signs and how to read them. We will also discuss four personality styles that you meet on the roadway everyday. Without the guidance of road signs, we might get lost along the way. How difficult life would be without the combination of signs and colored lights.

Years ago, my friend Marty and I decided to take a trip to Florida. However, we did not realize we were going on this trip until about an hour before the plane left. We were driving three friends to an Ohio airport to catch their flight to Orlando, Florida. During the drive, Marty and I could not stop wishing that we could go along. Our friends had their trip planned months in advance. They were staying in The Orlando Resort Hotel for two days and then they were off for a four-day cruise. During the entire ride to the airport, our friends were teasing us about the 90 degree weather, beaches, and nightclubs they would soon be enjoying. I began thinking about everything Florida had to offer as the temperature in Youngstown "dropped" another degree towards the freezing point.

We were running a bit late, so we decided to drop our friends off at the departure area. We told them we would park in short-term parking and meet them inside to bid them farewell. While exiting the departure area, we approached a fork in the road. The two signs staring at us read "Short-Term" parking, left, "Long-Term" parking, right. Marty and I looked at each other and in an instant, knew what the other was thinking. Without hesitation, I quickly turned the car to the right, heading for the Long-Term parking area.

After parking the car we went inside to meet our friends who were already boarding their flight. We did not mention where we parked, we just said, "See you soon!" Our friends boarded the plane and said they would see us in one week. Their plane wasn't even out of the gate yet when Marty and I rushed to the nearest ticket counter. We had no suitcases, suntan lotion, bathing suits, or anything else one usually packs for a trip to the "sunshine state." To make matters worse, the two of us could only come up with a total of $45 cash. The agent at the first counter explained that tickets purchased on this short of a notice would cost about $1,200 each. "Forget that," we said, and moved to the next agent where the situation was the same. We tried four or five different airlines before we found our lucky break. There was an airline running a weekend special and tickets were only $300 apiece, round trip. Finally a price that was under a grand. Marty and I looked at each other and said, "You only live once, let's go!"

We decided to use my credit card to purchase the tickets. Everything was falling into place. We were actually going through with this wild decision. Then like a bad dream, the agent said I would be over my credit limit if he put both tickets on my card. Because Marty had no credit card, we thought our adventure was over. Little did we know, it had just begun.

I immediately walked over to a pay phone and began to dial the credit card company to ask for an extended line of credit. There was no way I was going to let this opportunity pass us by. After about a half-hour (of really good motivational speaking) I was granted an extension. The adventure continued! We ran to the ticket counter and purchased two tickets for Orlando. You should have seen the look on the agent's face when he realized we had no carry on luggage *or* bags to check.

The "catch" with the cheaper tickets was that they were only good for weekend use. We would actually arrive in Florida Friday evening and have to leave early Sunday morning. We would only be basking in the warm sun for one full day. Such insanity!

When our plane finally landed we were excited. We needed a pay phone and we needed one quick. We wanted to reach our friends before they left their hotel room. Well, wouldn't you know it, on our way to find a phone, guess who we ran into? That's right, our friends! They could not believe their eyes when they saw us. To our advantage, we had bought tickets for a direct flight and they did not. Lady luck was surely shining on us that day. Our friends located their rental car, and of course, made room for two more. That vacation was one of the most bizarre I had ever experienced, and I loved every minute of it.

If we follow the same path, doing the same things day in and day out, our lives would become robotic rather than freestyle. Nothing should become too predictable. One must act in a carefree, happy-go-lucky manner once in a while and be spontaneous. To Marty and me, a little fun in the sun seemed a better prospect than returning to a shivering, freezing Ohio.

Every day we are faced with personal road signs telling us what we should or should not do. Make sure you take time to read and understand each sign, then proceed accordingly. The "Long-Term" parking sign that day told me to go have some fun and enjoy life. However, I had to read *between* the signs to figure it out.

Reading our personal road signs can sometimes be confusing. Have you ever had a "gut" feeling about something but you had no clue why? Perhaps you sensed you should drive to work using a different route, but you paid no mind to that feeling. You ended up in a tremendous traffic jam lasting two hours because you did not follow your instinct. Perhaps it was when you were sitting in the personnel office of a large corporation awaiting the interview for your dream job. It felt right when you started, however "something" told you not to take the position. Many people refer to this phenomenon as intuition. Call it what you will. My advice, follow it!

While in graduate school, I was working as a speaker/trainer for an independently owned and operated company. I thought I had finally hit the big time. Here I was, this young speaker working for this fabulous organization. This was my dream job. For the first few months, while getting my feet wet, I was feeling great. I was speaking to different companies about team building and leadership and was having a jolly good time. Suddenly, out of the blue, I began to feel restrictions being placed upon me. I was told how to speak, act, and train. Although I welcome advice or suggestions, these restrictions made me uncomfortable. How could I change my style? Certainly I could alter or tone down or up, but I was asked to change my whole being and who I was. I began feeling pressure to do things a specific way. Was it the wrong way? Not necessarily, but it proved to be the wrong way for me. After several weeks of self-talk and reading the signs, I decided to follow my gut and move forward.

During this time, I was living in a small apartment in Cleveland. A ten-minute bicycle ride from my residence would bring me to the shores of Lake Erie. When I needed a quiet place to release tension and be alone with my thoughts, many hours were spent relaxing near the cool, flowing waters. I love the water. It fascinates me to think there is another world functioning beneath the surface. Whenever I contemplated my future, I would go to my "special" spot on a large rock overlooking the water. No one bothered me. I could sit there and think for hours. It was my own little get-a-way.

One day at the water's edge, I made a gut decision that changed my life forever. I convinced myself to quit my job and start my own company. When I first thought this, I imagined I was nuts. Quit my job for real? Could I really do it? The answer was, Yes. The next day I handed in my resignation, leaving the company on good terms. I haven't regretted it since. Nothing in life comes easy, but most things can become easier. Have you read *your* road signs lately? Take every opportunity you get to visit your private place and recollect your thoughts.

Lets talk about your job for a moment. Are you completely happy with it? Do you wish you were doing something else? Are you complaining non-stop about how unhappy you are? These are not always easy questions to answer, but if you start reading your road signs and follow your intuition, they may become quite clear. I know you will not always love your job, in fact, there will probably even be days when you want to quit. That's normal. However, if the "bad" days begin to out number the "good" days, it may be time for a change. I can't tell you to quit your current job, but I can give you some darn good reasons why you *should* start looking for another.

If you are constantly in a bad mood, if you're becoming argumentative and short tempered, if you are depressed or feel stuck, it might be a good time to begin looking elsewhere for peace of mind. The pay may be less, but your attitude, outlook on life, and general health will definitely improve. Find something you like to do and make a career out of it.

Soap Opera Digest is a magazine familiarizing television viewers with all the daily diva happenings, and was created by a woman who enjoyed watching soap operas every day. My speaking business was started by someone who likes speaking, me. What do you feel passionate about? When you can answer that question, you my friend, may have just found a brand new career.

I read a fantastic article about a year ago in *USA Today*. The article title read: "Employees don't quit companies, they quit their boss!" How true this is. People do not usually quit their jobs because of the company, but instead, are leaving because they cannot get along with their supervisors. If you become your *own* boss, then you would have to quit *yourself.* By no means, am I saying you should run out and quit your job because you had a bad day. What I am saying is, we should be working to live, not *living* to work. Make the most of whatever situation you are in.

Our careers are not the only things that can make us happy or sad. What about your personal relationships? Are you reading the road signs there? If you are currently in a relationship that is constantly hitting potholes, then you might need to start reading those potholes as "signs." I believe the first step in solving a pothole filled relationship is to communicate with the other person. I do not just mean communicate, I mean COMMUNICATE. Talk to each other and discuss exactly what you both want and expect from your relationship. Find out specifically what makes one another tick and what bothers the other person. I am of the opinion that most everyday scuffles can be patched up through effective communication. If something is on your mind, express it. If your discussions are getting you nowhere, then perhaps, professional counseling should be explored. Never be too proud to admit you may need help. Not every relationship will be perfect. We are all aware of that. But, personal relationships, whether they are intimate or plutonic, can be fulfilling.

Allow me to share with you "Brian's Butterfly Theory," and how this theory has been a major road sign for me during my relationships with others. I have been using this butterfly theory for over 15 years, and it has yet to fail me. When I meet someone, I usually get an instantaneous feeling, comfortable or uncomfortable. When I meet someone who puts me at ease, I feel butterflies. When I meet someone with whom I have a *real* connection, the warm inner butterfly sensation becomes more than wonderful.

A perfect example of this is my relationship with my wife, Laura. I first met her when I was in the eighth grade. She was a younger student in my grade school and her mom, my mother-in-law, was the fifth grade teacher. Can you believe I married the fifth grade teacher's daughter! Actually, Laura and I never really spoke to each other often, but instead, were familiar faces along the corridors of our school. A few years ago, Laura admitted she had a crush on me while in grade school. In fact, she used to play house with her girlfriends and pretend she was married to me. What a woman! After graduation, Laura and I went our separate ways. This was an interesting turn of events as we separately drove down both rough, rocky roads and smooth pavements in life. Stories like this are common, but the endings are not always the same. Years went by and we each continued to do our own thing.

Then one magical night it happened. A few bachelor buddies and myself were out on the town when I suddenly noticed Laura. I got the butterflies. Boy, had she grown up *and* out, if you know what I mean! She was beautiful and I remember thinking, wow, this is the fifth grade teacher's daughter. My friends noticed my obvious attraction and encouraged me to say hello. What the heck, if I asked her for a date, all she could say was no, right? The moment I made the decision to walk towards her table, my roadway of life changed forever. We began talking, and the butterflies instantly fluttered in. This girl was great, and I didn't have to say it more than once to convince myself. We hit it off wonderfully that evening. After reminiscing the days of old, I asked for her telephone number. She said she would love if I called. Being a typical young man, I waited the appropriate time limit, back then, I think it was a three-day waiting period. When I finally decided to call her, I suddenly felt that "butterfly" feeling once again in my stomach. I was happy, nervous, and excited all wrapped into one. We spoke on the phone that evening for what seemed like hours, and the rest, as they say, is history.

We have spent many years together since then and the butterflies, I am happy to say, have increased for both of us. Are there days when the butterflies appear much stronger than other times? Of course, but the bottom line is they are still there and that makes all the difference in the world. My butterfly theory is simple, as you can see, but it has been a major road sign for not only myself, but my personal and professional relationships as well. When you can still feel butterflies of excitement and joy for a long period of time, even when you phone your wife from 750 miles away, you are receiving exactly what you need to travel along the path of life. Thank you, Laura, for keeping the butterflies alive.

If, for whatever reason, your butterflies have flown, then perhaps it is time to reassess your direction. Do you still feel those butterflies when you see that someone special? Is your career living up to the butterfly theory? I hope so. If not, then it might be time to expand your wings and fly away.

Let's chat for a moment about those traffic jams and how troublesome they can be. It never ceases to amaze me that traffic jams always occur when you are in a hurry. Personally, I have spent enough time sitting among those jams that I could have learned to speak a foreign language. On the contrary, I have used strong word power I never knew existed in my vocabulary before, so let's just say I have already been speaking a different language. You know when you travel, traffic jams are, and always will be, a part of life.

When roads are bumpy and in extremely poor condition, we want them repaired. While they are being fixed, we want the traffic jams to disappear. I know you have heard this phrase before, but it definitely applies here, "You can't have your cake and eat it too!"…or can you? I suppose one could say traffic jams are God's way of advising all drivers to take some time to stop and smell the roses. Many may not think in this manner, but maybe we should. There is too much to see and do in life. Why let a personal traffic jam keep you from taking a little time out to "jam" with your family, go on a picnic, have fun, teach your children patience as well as love. Time with your loved ones, doing something for your family, that's what life should be about.

While you are sitting in highway traffic jams, check the gas gauge. Do you have a full tank? Then yell out as loud as you can, I'VE GOT GAS! You can then break out in a song, talk to yourself, car dance, call someone you love on the cell phone, or perhaps take a moment to observe any scenery around. You would be surprised at how much beauty surrounds you if you would simply take the time to look. If there is an accident, be thankful you are not involved and while you wait for traffic to move, say a prayer for those who were. When you practice patience, you are actually providing yourself with GAS.

I travel frequently and have had the unfortunate opportunity of experiencing a great number of traffic jams. In fact, there is "sooooooo" much road construction on our nation's highways, I think the government should consider changing every state tree to an orange barrel! I actually believe I see *more* orange barrels and cones on the road than I do state trees.

On the highway, traffic jams and detours are within viewing distance. What about the personal jams in your life, are they visible? When stopped in a traffic jam, you can always pop your head out the window and take a peek at the action up ahead. What about the action that lies ahead in your personal life? Have you altered your direction in life by taking a detour? When I was stuck in my old job, I felt as though I was sitting in a never-ending traffic jam. I finally did something about it, and you can, too. I must remind you to always have faith in whatever you do, believe in yourself, and take that detour around whatever traffic jam is holding you back!

Mothers, fathers, brothers, sisters, cousins, friends, lovers, co-workers, and clients, to name a few, serve as road signs in our lives. Our family and friends can be "traffic lights" along the road. Sometimes they become our green, red, and yellow lights in order to help guide us down the road to our projected destinations. When we are cruisin' through life too fast, we might need them to be red. When we are cruisin' too slowly, maybe they should be green. And still at other times, they can act as yellow "caution" lights.

Be very careful when that yellow (caution) light comes within your viewing distance. If you hurry through, you may be taking an un-necessary risk. Always gently step on the brake and assess the situation. Once you have thought things through and are ready to make a move, accelerate! Do not hesitate! Here are a few yellow light situations you might currently be facing: Get married—do not get married; quit your job—stick with your job; apologize—do not apologize; ask for the raise—do not ask for the raise; spend extra time with the kids and family—do not spend extra time with the kids and family; buy the house—do not buy the house; eat the chocolate cake—do not eat the chocolate cake; buy the new car—do not buy the new car; cut the grass—do not cut the grass; hold a grudge—do not hold a grudge. The list goes on and on. Life is full of yellow light moments and the choices you make during those moments could make or break your destiny. Knowing when to hit the brakes or apply the gas is your decision. Maximize your yellow light opportunities, or before you know it, you could be facing a life of red lights stopping you at every turn.

Now, let's discuss respect for one's self and others. When you are able to love and respect yourself, you will be able to love and respect others. Loving yourself does not have to be a vanity thing. You can love yourself and just as easily break up with yourself. Certainly you have heard the statement, "You should treat people the way you treat yourself." I find it a little difficult to digest that tidbit all the time. If you dislike who you are, you will send negative vibrations. This could definitely cause trouble along the road. Taking care of *yourself* should be the first priority on your list of things to do. However, most people believe that they are being self-centered and egotistical if they look out for themselves first. You are only being self-centered if, once you look out for yourself, you *forget* to look out for others.

Here is a wonderful example that a colleague of mine, John, uses during his presentations. Imagine that you are flying on an airplane with your child. If you do not have children, imagine someone else you love. You have boarded the flight and are settled in your assigned seat as the flight attendants recite their pre-flight checklist. They instruct you on the use of your seatbelts, explain what to do in case of a water landing, and where the exit doors are located. Finally they explain that the oxygen mask will drop from the ceiling due to severe pressure changes. They tell you, when the mask drops, YOU should put *yours* on <u>first</u>. Our foremost reaction would be to assist our child or loved one, but we are advised against this. Why? They want *you* to be in good condition so that you can more effectively help others. That makes sense to me.

Have you ever been cruisin' down the street and all of a sudden had to slam on the brakes? If you had a passenger in the seat next to you, what was your first response? Chances are you stretched your arm out to stop the passenger from going forward. This was a reaction. It is natural for us to want to help others, which is very good, but be certain you look out for yourself as well.

Let me share with you one of my philosophies. I believe you need to start kissing your own butt at every opportunity you get. That's right, smooch away. Too many times we go through life kissing everyone else's, however, when it comes time to kiss our own, we have no pucker left in our lips. Sometimes when we are in the presence of our boss's, we subconsciously kiss butt. We smile and do the "booty smooch." Then as soon as they leave, we mumble under our breath how much we'd like to *kick* their butt. The next time you feel you're about to "pucker up" for someone else, think about laying a wet one on yourself first!

Listening is another road sign of life. It could demonstrate that you care and are interested in others. Many times, we actually pretend to listen during interpersonal communication. This could reveal that you are bored and uninterested. The person perceives we are listening, but our minds are somewhere else in "la-la land." Have you ever "fake-listened" to someone? You probably have. Everyone has been guilty of this at one time or another, perhaps during driver education class. You more than likely ignored the instructor, yawning as you stated under your breath, "Yeah right." Your head was shaking up and down as if you were paying attention, but you weren't hearing a thing. Undoubtedly, most of our driving lecture sessions were spent in fake-listening mode.

Clap your hands three times right now. Did you hear the noise they made? If you answered yes, you should give thanks. *Hearing*, one of your five senses, is a gift, given to you at birth. *Listening*, on the other hand, is *not* a gift, but rather, an acquired skill. The ability to *truly* listen is a beautiful thing. When was the last time you actually used that particular skill?

The remainder of this Mile Marker is dedicated to the four general personalities with which we communicate daily. The study of human beings and their personality traits has fascinated scholars for many centuries and will continue to for years to come.

Psychologists have created numerous tests and methods to measure behavioral differences. Some tests have an excellent rating system while others have no rating system at all, although they often seem closely related. Self-analysis surveys can categorize individuals into as many as 16 different personalities, while others maintain that there are only two. What makes one survey better than the other? It is not the actual test that is either good or bad, but rather the manner in which the information and results are presented. Some are too lengthy and confusing, while others are too short and uninformative. My goal in this section is to encourage awareness of your own personality and the personalities of those you meet every day.

Let me introduce you to the Dominator, Evaluator, Actor, and Harmonizer, a.k.a. the 4x4/SUV, Volvo, Sports Car, and Minivan. Each personality has specific characteristics and attributes. First we'll discuss their behaviors. Then I'm going to explain how to communicate effectively with each. Just as we learn the symbols and meanings of each road sign and traffic light, we should also have the ability to understand individual people.

When you get into your car and start the engine, you have the precise key. If you do not have the exact grooved metal implement to fit your automobile, it will not ignite. The same concept applies to people. If you do not use the "key" elements to connect with others, their engines will not engage either.

I have, in the interest of fun, selected certain vehicles for each personality. These are what *I* imagine each particular personality would drive if given the choice. If you drive a make of car that does not match the personality or vice versa, do not panic.

During a motivational address, I was explaining each of the personalities and what car I pictured them driving. It was merely a fun experiment, but one woman in the audience took me too seriously. After the presentation, she approached the stage in a rather unpleasant manner.

Shaking her finger, she said, "I can't believe you! I drive a minivan and I am nothing like that personality you described. I consider myself to be more like the 4x4/SUV."

"Ah, excuse me, ma'am, but as I said earlier, this was merely an experiment. I reminded the audience, if you drive a certain car that does not match your particular personality please don't be angry. I chose to use examples at random which I believed would not offend anyone. I apologize if you are upset. Perhaps you did not *hear* me state this was just an example?"

"Well, I guess I didn't understand."

"Tell me something," I asked. "You would describe yourself as a 4x4/SUV, right?"

"Most assuredly so!"

"Well then, I would have to agree with your self diagnosis because the downfall of the 4x4/SUV is poor listening." She and I both laughed.

Keep in mind that you are actually *all* four personalities and each characteristic is not always 100 percent true. For example, I know many Dominators who are exceptional listeners, which happens to be their greatest downfall. At any given time you can switch gears. I firmly believe we all have that *one* particular personality which stands out a bit more than the rest. Sit back, read, and absorb the information, then decide for yourself which personality describes you best.

Dominators are individuals who like things short, sweet, and to the point! Sometimes they make poor listeners while involved in conversations. When Dominators are having a conversation with someone and they received the information they were looking for, while the other person continues to talk, Dominators will tune them out with a "fake" listen. This personality prefers control, but that does not mean *they* have to be in control. For example, when the Dominator goes to a meeting, he or she wants it to start on time. They want everything covered. They want out on time. They do not care if the tooth fairy is controlling the meeting, as long as it's controlled. If control however, is lost, during any one session, they will step in and take over. Can you guess what Dominators would be most worried about while playing a basketball game? If you said "winning," you are correct. Winning is the main attitude occupying their mind. Dominators like goals. In a team environment, they will make sure goals are being *set*. Dominators are more like 4x4/SUV's because they are sturdy, tough, and will get you where you have to go. Dominators, we love you!

THE DOMINATOR

Characteristics/Attributes

• Direct
• Bottom line/no beating around the bush
• Likes controlled situations
• Goal oriented
• Give them info, then get lost

Motivator = Winning

Downfall = Poor listening

Favorite Car = SUV/4x4 (move it or lose it)

Favorite Movie = King Kong

Personalized License Plate =

Evaluators are people who like to think things through. When Evaluators go to an amusement park and they ride the double-loop roller coaster, the first thing out of their mouth is, "Wow, that was *interesting*. How fast do you think we had to be traveling in order for us not to fall out of our seats?" They enjoy the ride, but are *more* interested in trying to figure out the process that makes the ride run smoothly. Dominators would have gotten off the ride and said, "Cool, next ride please!" Evaluators can never just *jump* into a car and take a road trip. First, they must turn on their computers and type in MapQuest.com. Next, they check the oil and fill the gas tank. Until everything is planned and taken care of, they will not be able to start their journey. As you will soon discover, Actors have no problem with taking impulse road trips and would have answered, "Who cares where we go, let's just go!"

What do you think the Evaluators main focus is while playing in a basketball game? If you said numbers and statistics, you are correct. Evaluators like to win, but they are actually more worried about their strategy and statistics. When they are on the free throw line, the only thing running through their minds is that they have to be five for five tonight or else their perfect "stats" will be off. They do want a victory, but again, it might not be their first priority. There are many reasons why Evaluators perform things in a slow manner. Many believe it is due to the fact that they are perfectionists. Because of this, they have a difficult time making decisions. They want to be sure the choices being made are the *right* ones. In a team environment, the Evaluator will make certain goals are being **met**. Evaluators think things through before purchasing anything, and prefer to drive Volvo's because they are safe, reliable, and economical on gas. Evaluators, we love you!

THE EVALUATOR

Characteristics/Attributes
- Likes the facts
- Loves statistics
- Precise
- Thinker
- Wants to know, WHY??

Motivator = Accuracy

Downfall = Slow

Favorite Car = Volvo (I know you can, I know you can)

Favorite Movie = Documentary on Einstein's Theory of Relativity

Personalized License Plate =

Actors like things to be fun and exciting. If there is an opportunity for them to be the class clown, they will take it. This personality can entice others to "open" up. For example, if you are at a party and you do not know someone across the room, the Actor will walk you over and make an introduction. "Bob this is Sally, Sally this is Bob, let's all go get a drink." When Actors are sitting among an audience of 6,000 people and the speaker requests a few volunteers, they will be the first person to jump out of their seat, raise their hand and say, "Take me, take me!" Evaluators will just sit there, not making any attempt to volunteer. But instead, will wonder *why* the speaker might need a volunteer. The Dominator will push the person sitting next to them and say, "Raise your hand!" A bit silly, but true.

If Actor's were playing in a basketball game, what do you think their main focus would be? If you said "crowd/fans," you are correct. Actors do want to win and they are worried about their statistics, but they are *more* concerned with pleasing the audience. They know people are watching them, therefore they feel the need to put on a good show. They may go as far as changing the color of their hair for each game. Actors tend to be somewhat disorganized. They usually have 50 things going on at once.

There are moments when they become confused. If you will note the next time you speak with someone in this category, after only two minutes of conversation, they can bring up as many as 30 different subjects. In a team environment, the Actor is the one making sure the team is having *fun* while achieving their goals. Actors are like little sports cars because they are fast, quick, and generally sharp in appearance. Actors, we love you!

THE ACTOR

Characteristics/Attributes
- Likes to have fun
- Very dynamic
- Risk taker/go getter
- High energy
- Talkative

Motivator = An audience

Downfall = Disorganized

Favorite Car = Sports Car (fast, faster, fastest)

Favorite Movie = Cannon Ball Run

Personalized License Plate =

Harmonizers feel good when they know the people around them are secure and happy. This personality is very supportive and nurturing. When you are invited to their home, they will cater to your every need. Their homes, every room, will be in *Home and Garden* shape. Candles will be lit. Special towels will be hanging in the bathroom, the works. They will constantly ask, "Do you want this, do you want that, are you hot, are you cold? Here try this because I baked it just for you!" When Harmonizers are entertaining friends, they are the hosts who are considerate of your wants and needs. They will stock the refrigerator with soda, wine, iced tea, lemonade, and Kool-Aid (every flavor) just in case someone might request it.

Actors are a little different and, to avoid anyone noticing the clutter, will throw anything from clothes to garbage lying around the house into one room and lock the door. No one goes in that room. (This sounds a little familiar to me!) Harmonizers cannot possibly do that. They are great people, but they let themselves get taken advantage of occasionally. Here's a secret, so listen closely. Harmonizers have a little black book. The day you offend them, you may not even know they are upset, but when they go home that night watch out, because chances are, you have just been penciled into their black book! Can you get out? Yes, but you do have to build up their trust once again. Sorry Harmonizers if I let the "cat out of the bag," please don't pencil me in. Can you guess what Harmonizers would be focused on most while playing a basketball game? If you said the "losing" team, you are correct. In a team environment, this personality creates *peace* while working on goals. Harmonizers drive Minivan's just in case someone else needs a ride. Harmonizers, we love you!

THE HARMONIZER

Characteristics/Attributes

• Best listener

• Very caring

• Nurturing

• Uses sympathy/empathy

• Cry on their shoulder

Motivator = Security

Downfall = Allows self to get taken advantage of
(and shame on us for doing it)

Favorite Car = Minivan (You need a ride? Come with me!)

Favorite Movie = Lassie

Personalized License Plate =

Well, what do you think? Did you have bells ringing ding-a-ling-a-ling while you were reading? You should have, because I just described your employer, co-workers, clients, spouse, lover, friends, children, relatives, and you. Never forget, that our personalities can shift from situation to situation, but we all posses one which usually stands above the rest. Knowing the four personalities' strengths and weaknesses will help you effectively communicate with others. This can make your life much easier personally and professionally.

Before I share with you some great strategies on how to connect with each personality and learn how to "key" into their ignitions, I want to describe two more examples. This should provide you with more insight as to how the 4x4/SUV, Volvo, Sports Car, and Minivan think. I ask that you kindly follow through and play along as you think about what you might do in the following situation.

Please imagine you are in a grocery store. You are standing in a checkout line that is 10 people deep. There are a total of eight registers, however, there is only **one** open and that's the line you're standing in. What would you be doing in line? If you said getting the manager, you may be a Dominator. The Dominator is the personality who will get out of the long line, walk over to the manager and boldly complain. "There are too many people waiting in one line. You have eight registers, let's get some help out here before I drive my 4x4/SUV right through the store." However, before leaving, the Dominator will always find the Harmonizer personality and ask them to hold their place in line.

If you said you would be looking for another register to open, you may be an Evaluator. Evaluators have hawk eyes and know another register is going to open soon. It would seem they know exactly how many people are working that day and what time everyone takes a break. They are the first person to see new cashiers walking with their drawers of cash towards a middle line. The Evaluator can look for a new line, balance the checkbook, and still find time to read a magazine. Evaluators have also been known to count up other people's groceries. They will attempt to estimate how long they will have to be in line according to how many things each person has in their buggy. If you are ever caught in an express lane with more than 10 or 12 items, it is probably safe to say an Evaluator has caught you.

If you imagined you would be talking with others, then you just might be the Actor personality. Actors would look at this situation and say, "A captive audience not going anywhere!" These are the individuals who start interacting with others, telling jokes, and are just having a grand old time. There're putting on a show for everyone else to watch.

Finally, if you are the sweet Harmonizer, then you are the only person in line who actually feels bad for the poor cashier who must check-out the angry customers. This personality will let others "cut" in line if they have fewer items. Harmonizers have also been known to help bag the groceries, but so have Dominators, Evaluators, and Actors. Harmonizers bag the groceries because they know the cashier could use a little help. Dominators help bag the groceries because they do not like the way the bag person is doing it. Evaluators help bag the groceries because they know they'll get out quicker. And the Actor is helping to bag the groceries simply to say, "Hey, look at me! I'm bagging!" The next time you are in the supermarket I hope you think of your author and this analogy.

Here is another example of the personalities in action. Imagine that our four personalities have just approached a four-way stop at the same time. Who is the first person through? If you said 4x4/SUV, you are correct. Dominators don't even stop, they just slow down a bit, then "vrooooooom" right through. The next person to make a move could be any of the three, but I am going to guess it is the Volvo. The Evaluator looks right, looks left, and then says "Too close to call," and puts the car in reverse to find another route.

Next to make a move are the Sports Cars. They however, are not moving forward, but instead, are moving *in* their car. Actors are singing and car dancing. They are checking out others and their rides before they eventually decide to move forward. The last person stuck at the four-way stop is the good old Minivan. Why? Because Harmonizers are the ones with their hands out the window, waving along the other cars to proceed in front of them. If you are smiling, then you have been there and done that. Remember, all four personalities are wonderful, just different.

Now that we have a background on each personality, let's take a look at the "Key" Factor. As mentioned earlier, certain keys are required to start certain cars. A Sports Car key will not start a Volvo and a Minivan key will not fit into a 4x4/SUV. Wouldn't the same apply to all of us? There are certain key elements to remember when communicating with each personality. What key starts which car is important to know. Keep in mind that *your* key characteristics may differ from another.

When communicating with Dominators (4x4/SUV) you need to share their ignition key to create a comfort zone. There are many characteristics you should remember about the Dominator. Keep the conversation short, sweet, and to the point. Do not drag the conversation out. Make sure the 4x4/SUV heard what you said. Be very direct with them, as they will appreciate it. Evaluators (Volvo) like things to be explained in great detail. When communicating with this personality remember that the key to their ignition is accuracy. Bar graphs and pie charts are absolutely acceptable when dealing with Evaluators. They enjoy things described slowly, so give it to them in that manner.

Actors (Sports Car) prefer things to be exciting. The proper key to start their engine and connect with them, is to have fun! Do not use detailed descriptions and have lengthy conversations. If you were to use a bar graph or pie chart, you would probably confuse them. Actors are high-energy people and they appreciate it when others can keep up with their speed. Finally, you have the Harmonizers (Minivan). The number one key to use in order to start their ignition is to be the best listener possible. These people enjoy listening, therefore, they enjoy being listened to. Do not be harsh with this personality, instead, choose to utilize more compassion and patience. They are people who will go out of their way for you, but keep in mind it is not in your interest to take advantage of them, unless you want to end up in their little black book.

If you desire more information about these four personalities, I recommend a fabulous book titled *The Platinum Rule*. This book was written by Tony Alessandra, Ph.D. and Michael J. O'Connor, Ph.D. The Platinum Rule is simply this: "Do unto others as *they'd* like done unto them." This rule shows you how to treat people the way *they* would like to be treated. When you find yourself interacting with a specific personality, remember to use the right "key" to start their engine.

THE <u>KEY</u> FACTOR

Keys that "start" each personality engine

Dominator (4x4/SUV) ....*Be direct, short, sweet, and to the point. Say what you need to say and move on.*

Evaluator (Volvo) .... *Be more detailed with your communication. Try to be as accurate as possible.*

Actor (Sports Car) .... *Make things fun for this person. Keep your energy as high as possible.*

Harmonizer (Minivan) .... *Be gentle. Listen attentively to this personality and make them feel safe and secure.*

This third Mile Marker was designed to make you aware of the signs that guide your life. Are you following them correctly? Do you know what detours are up ahead? Have you faced a personal yellow "caution" light situation lately? Are your keys starting the right engines? When life seems confusing, learn to read between the signs.

CRUISIN' CONCEPTS TO CONSIDER...

- *Start reading life's little road signs*

- *Yellow (caution) light moments happen quickly*

- *Take detours*

- *Brian's Butterfly Theory*

- *The KEY Factor*

  (4x4/SUV, Volvo, Sports Car, Minivan)

SLOW

END **35** SPEED LIMIT

DO NOT ENTER

YIELD

STOP

PIT STOPS AND
OIL CHANGES

"Always do your best. What you plant now, you will harvest later."

- OG Mandino

Have you ever had a mentor? If you answered yes, then you know what benefits can come from this relationship. If you answered no, you may want to reconsider your answer. I would like you to try something for a moment. This exercise is called "Positive Pit-Crew." Notice the three columns below. Each column is labeled with a subtitle: teacher, supervisor, and friend.

TEACHER	SUPERVISOR	FRIEND

Think of a teacher you especially liked, one who influenced you in a positive way. It could be your second grade teacher, a high school teacher, college professor or any teacher at all. There have been many teachers throughout our lives, some top quality and others who couldn't teach us how to spell c-a-t without spending an hour explaining the why, when, and where we can use this word. Boring indeed! It does not matter where they taught or for how long. Please insert his/her name. Now, think about the various jobs you have held. Who were your supervisors? Write down the name of your favorite.

Who do you trust most? Who is always there for you when you need them? If you were about to fall from a high mountain peak, this person would save you. Please write down your "best" friend's name. (Don't overlook the friendships in your own family.)

Look over the names you have listed. Guess what? These people did something **right**! You could have picked any teacher in the world, but POW, that person came to mind. You could have picked any supervisor or friend, but the two you wrote down obviously influenced you in some outstanding manner. Why did they make your list? What did they do that made them so memorable?

At this time, list their particular characteristics and attributes. You will notice that the lists may be similar. Perhaps your "crew" served as interested listeners and were very enthusiastic about life. Maybe they had a great smile or made you laugh. Whatever they did, write it down. Review what you just wrote. If you stated you never had a mentor before, guess what? News Flash…Here They Are. A mentoring relationship does not have to be, "Hey, you're my mentor, sign this piece of paper." We all have mentoring relationships from which we can grow and learn.

As a tool for learning, I have a challenge for you. Each morning, pick <u>one</u> particular behavior from your list and "model" it all day long.

The next morning, and every morning after, repeat the process. If you accept this "daily challenge" and sincerely apply it to your life, you will not be disappointed. In fact, it is inevitable that *you* may one-day serve on someone *else's* Pit-Crew. It's never too late to start!

Professional racecar drivers depend on their pit-crews to keep them safe in many ways. They provide everything from encouragement to tire changes. All must be done with an efficient, positive attitude, no matter how the crew feels before a particular race. Drivers must feel confident in their pit-crew, ensuring safety and security.

Learning from others is a powerful thing, but the most important chore you have yet to face is the power to apply and utilize what you have learned. When was the last time you visited *your* crew in the pit stop?

About three years ago I was in my first automobile accident. The accident took place in Cleveland. No one was injured, but there was a considerable amount of damage to my car. My hometown, as mentioned earlier, was Youngstown. Not being entirely familiar with the Cleveland area and its mass variety of mechanics, I decided to bring the car back to Youngstown for repair. I fortunately remembered someone telling me about a business called The Himrod Company. I had never been there and knew nothing about its reputation. Because I needed the car to be professionally repaired within a short period of time, I decided to give it a try. That decision, on that day, allowed me to add two more members to my Positive Pit-Crew.

From the moment I walked through the door as a complete stranger, Bert Toth Jr. and his father, Bert Sr., were kind and helpful. They were two of the best customer service representatives I had ever met. They led me into their office and offered me a good cup of hot coffee and cookies *before* they even knew my identity. After all, I could have been there to sell them encyclopedias for all they knew! While I was in their presence, we spoke for quite some time, getting to know one another on a personal, first name basis. I learned how their business began and exchanged some facts about myself.

When I finally showed them the damage to my vehicle, within moments they gave me a fair and reasonable estimate. It seemed there would be a complete and satisfactory recovery, with my car looking as good as new and running 100 percent safely. They were honest and sincere regarding my car's overall prognosis. It would become their first priority. They asked if I would like them to fix it, or instead, shop around. I told them, "You had me at cookies, you had me at cookies!" Within two days, as promised, I was driving back to Cleveland. Since then, I have been back a dozen times. Every time I return, I am treated with the same kindness and generosity. Once in a while I make it a point to take some time merely to visit these fine folks, bringing them, you guessed it…cookies.

Along with being a motivational speaker, I am also a trainer/consultant. During my years as a trainer, I have conducted hundreds of customer service seminars throughout the United States. Let me tell you, these two gentlemen could have taught classes 10 times better than me, or any other trainer for that matter.

Thanks Bert Jr. and Bert Sr. for showing me the true meaning of excellent customer service. (By the way, if you're driving through the Youngstown area and your car starts giving you problems, may I recommend The Himrod Company.)

Most of us are comfortable with a limited basic knowledge of our cars. For example, do you know where the oil goes? Can you change your own spark plugs? What about replacing your brakes? If you answered yes to any of these questions, I commend you for knowing how. If you answered no, I can only say, "It's OK." You do not necessarily need to know everything about cars and their engines. That's why we pay mechanics.

In life we are faced with similar circumstances. There will always be situations in which we have no interest. Having someone on your pit-crew who *does*, is a good idea.

One of my closest friends, Bob (murphbear), a computer genius, is one of the individuals on my Positive Pit-Crew. I know nothing about the inner workings of the computer, nor do I have the knowledge of all the software, bells and whistles, or voices that come through my speaker. I can turn it on and type, use the e-mail and Internet, then turn it off again. Computers are a great invention, making things easier for those in business or anyone simply using them for pleasure.

I was leery about purchasing a computer, but with Bob's assistance, I felt comfortable with the process. He was the member of my pit-crew who proved to be more suitable for decision making on my behalf by advising me which computer to buy. He explained what programs best suited my needs and how to use the ever-so-puzzling equipment that was installed within.

Let's reverse the roles for a moment. When Bob has a speech to deliver, guess who he calls first? What goes around, comes around. Thanks Bob for being there when I needed a pit stop.

When you take your vehicle into one of those businesses that advertise 10-minute oil changes, do you know what they do? The mystery is over. They check: chassis lubrication, oil filter, spark plugs and gaskets, tire pressure, brake fluid, power steering fluid, antifreeze level, window wiper washer fluid, air filter, PCV valve, cooling system, radiator cap, transaxle, serpentine belt, and last but not least, they change the oil. Pretty impressive! It is amazing that they do this in about the same time it takes us to wash our face, comb our hair, and brush our teeth.

Cars require service all the time, and so do we in order to maintain our lives. You are an engine and need to make certain you are running in tip-top shape. When was the last time you serviced yourself?

Are you sticking to that diet? Are you saving money each month in accordance with your plans? Are you spending time with your family? All of the aforementioned things require time and attention. If you don't routinely check your gauges, you may find yourself in the repair shop. Who knows how long that could last? Make sure you continue to "service" the important things in your life. The human engine cannot be changed in 10 minutes and some of the repairs from previous "wreckage" may take much longer. Take time for that approximate "3,000 mile" self tune-up. It's a must!

Pit stops remind me of something that most people fear, change. If it makes you uncomfortable, you're not alone. Most people dread change. The number one reason many of us fear it is because when we have to do something *different*, our first thought is, "Oh phooey, we have to do it *this* way because the way we have been doing it in the *past* has been wrong." It's wrong to think this way. Having to change does not mean you have been doing something wrong, it just means you're attempting something different. When the Model T was invented in the early 1900's, it transferred people from Point A to Point B. The 2002 models are doing the same thing. You are still traveling from Point A to Point B, however, you are doing it with more style and comfort. The automobile has evolved throughout the years and will continue its evolution into the future. **Change** paves the way for **opportunity**.

Years ago, a participant in one of my seminars was adamant about change, stating that anything "different" was bad. For approximately five minutes I tried to persuade him otherwise, but he would not listen to anything I had to say. His attitude was actually beginning to bring the positive atmosphere of the entire seminar down. I was getting nowhere fast, so I acted quickly. I reached into my wallet and pulled out a $20 bill, gave it to the man without looking at his face, and kept right on talking to the audience. Everyone seemed confused. I kept on speaking.

After 15 minutes had passed, I looked at John and asked him in a jovial manner, "Did you find the fact that I gave you a $20 bill just for the fun of it, bad?"

He snickered. "No, of course not."

"Good," I said. "Now let me ask you another question. Do people normally walk up to you and give you $20 bills?"

"Of course not!"

"So you're telling me that receiving $20 was something different and it was not bad?"

"I already told you…." His face turned red as the ton of bricks fell upon him. He had something different happen to him that was actually not bad. I said nothing more to him for the remaining part of the seminar. Afterwards, he came up to me and returned the $20 bill. "Thanks for the lesson. Best tip I ever got!"

Accepting change is sometimes a slow procedure. Therefore, our internal brakes need to be applied before we rush into a judgement regarding this issue. Begin thinking about the positive things that change can create.

When automobiles were first invented little thought was given to brakes. The emphasis was on getting the car to move, not on stopping it. Although the Flintstones had already perfected braking, not too many of us were willing to scrape our feet on the ground until we stopped. Over time, technology improved and brakes became as important as the gas pedal. It took a few accidents before we discovered what caused the trouble. It seems people did not notice when their brakes began to wear out. No one realized that constantly pressing and pumping the brake pedal down to the floorboard was indeed, a bad thing. Eventually, when the driver least expected it, the brakes would "go out."

This was a potentially dangerous problem. Manufacturers began to place a small strip of metal, a "screech strip," on the brake pad.

When the pad wore down, the piece of metal would make contact with the rotor, causing a terribly annoying SCREEEEEECH sound every time you made an attempt to stop. Enlightened drivers would then know it was time to change the brakes. Others would simply turn up the radio!

We need to begin listening to our *own* internal screech strips. How are your internal brakes holding up? Do you need new pads? How many times have you ignored your brakes and went straight for the gas? Next time you're cruisin' through life at 150 mph and haven't a clue as to why you are traveling that fast, do not forget your internal screech strip. At a very young age, we learned to stop, look, and listen before crossing the street. As we grow older, we slow down, glance, and go. Change your brake pads every other day if needed.

In the early 1980's a law was passed that required every automobile to be equipped with a three-inch brake light, in the rear window or on the trunk. This law passed for obvious reasons. Accidents were occurring entirely too often, so the "third" brake light was added.

As you continue to travel through life, make certain all of your brake and headlights are visible. Slow down, observe all signs and watch for others' lights as well. You do not want to cause an accident simply because you did not spend enough time on your own lighting system. If your inner lights are working properly, your body engine is purring, and you have an internal full tank of GAS, then you are in great shape.

Our cars speak to us everyday. Whether it is the screech strips "screeeeeeching" or the car horns "hoooooonking," our vehicles are speaking. Next time you drive, count the number of times you hear a horn beep. Annoying isn't it? It's as though you were in a quiet room and all of a sudden you can hear the light bulb buzzing. It's been buzzing since you entered the room, but you did not notice it. Once you are aware of the sound, it can drive you "bonkers." As we cruise, we sometimes need to listen to our own horns blasting at others. We can annoy others just as they at times annoy us. The phrase, "Don't toot your own horn too loudly," applies to all of us at one time or another. Am I saying you should not be proud of yourself and your accomplishments? Of course not, it's simply that without realizing it, we may be talking about ourselves *too* much.

If you want to build a great rapport with someone, show a genuine interest in them, rather than yourself. Talking about our one and only self is simple to do, but guard against monopolizing the conversation. Give others the "spotlight" and your full attention. This will result in creating a strong comfort zone. When someone tells you a story they are proud of and you have a similar or much better one, save it. If you tell your story, it may deflate theirs. If someone finds a $5 bill and is excited, postpone your story about finding a $10 bill for another time. Let others have the glory every once in a while.

"Smoke screening" is a negative communication tactic used by many. When a vehicle has white or black smoke billowing from the tailpipe, this smoke screen becomes distracting. Whether you are with a co-worker or a family member, be alert to smoke screening. This form of manipulative communication is harmful to both parties involved. When you make an attempt to hurt or cheat someone, tell a lie or back stab, you are smoke screening. This depletes GAS from your self-esteem tank.

Another popular car noise is the "squeaky" fan belt. The squeaky fan belt noise is very annoying and could actually be embarrassing to the driver of the automobile. What's funny is, when it happens to us, we quickly act as though it's coming from another direction. Busted again.

If we aren't careful with our tone of voice and how we converse with others, we can sound exactly like the squeaky fan belt. Constant complaining, squeak, squeak, squeak, blah, blah, blah, could lead you into the valley of the squeaky fan belt. The next time you feel like whining, stop for a moment and listen to yourself squeak.

Let's chat for a moment about the hypnotic rhythm of the windshield wipers. Wipers are made to go back and forth, back and forth, back and forth, thus enabling us to observe everything with much more clarity. Rain, snow, sleet, and hail are no match for the windshield wipers. In our personal lives, when we are confronted with similar "elements," we must remember to switch on our wipers and look at things from a "new" perspective. Some people cruise blindly, failing to see anything in its proper perspective simply because they have so much "guck" on their windshield of life, it obstructs their vision. If you begin to witness some negative particles hindering your insight, try using your washer fluid. We need our "systems" running smoothly. Remember, *"The choices you make today, will affect <u>someone</u> tomorrow."*

Tom, a dear friend of mine throughout high school and college, cruised through life enjoying the scenery every step of the way. He maintained a positive outlook, never smoke screening others, blowing his horn too loudly, or squeaking in frustration. Because he treated others with exceptional kindness, he earned the title of, "the guy everyone loved being with." He was blessed with a pleasant personality and a priceless smile. I wish Tom could have helped me proofread this book, but he passed away eight years ago before the world really had the chance to know him. No one can predict exactly why things happen the way they do.

One night after leaving work, he accepted a ride from an inebriated co-worker. He became a passenger with no control. That yellow caution light moment changed the course of his life forever. The driver had nothing operating properly within his system. His internal brakes were shot and he disregarded his screech strip. His wiper blades were off, his inner light was dull, and he was subconsciously smoke screening. His internal engine was in the "shut down" mode.

To this day, we still do not know why the car swerved off the road. The driver has to live with the fact that he killed someone because of his drunkenness. Tom's decision affected him, his family, and his friends. Make sure *your* life choices will affect you and others in a positive way. Stay in shape and keep alert!

Tune-ups in life and positive thinking are essential, but there are those who would disagree. Have you ever met a negative Nelly, rotten Randy, or a gloom and doom personality? These individuals see the downside of everything. If you gave them a whole lemon, they would complain there was no knife to cut it.

Studies have shown that about 80 percent of our daily thoughts tend to be negative. Scary isn't it? Thinking negatively, by the way, does not mean we're thinking horrible thoughts, just not positive ones. Let me give you a few examples. When you're approaching a traffic light, you probably never think to yourself, "It's going to stay green," instead you think, "It's going to turn red, I just know it's going to turn red before I get there!" How about when you purchase that birthday present you spent so much time picking out? In the mall you thought the person you were buying it for would love it, now, as he or she begins tearing away at the wrapping, you're sitting in the corner thinking to yourself, "They're not going to like it." It seemed like a perfect gift in the store, but *now,* you're not so sure. What about the performance review at work? I highly doubt when it's your turn you happily sprint into the room and request that proverbial raise. Chances are you're wondering, "What are they going to find wrong with my work performance *this* time?" What are your first thoughts in the morning when you wake up and realize you have to get ready for work?

It is absolutely true we all possess some negative thinking. If you *think* negatively, you might *communicate* negatively. We may be speaking to our colleagues in a negative manner without even realizing it. "Hey Fred, I know you don't really like team building, but too bad. This is what we are doing here and if you don't shape up, you'll be shipped out.

You *won't* get your raise if you're not on the team!" Perhaps at home you speak to your children in the same a way, "Hey Bobby, if you don't eat your broccoli, you're *not* getting dessert," or "Hey Susie, if you don't clean your room, you're *not* going to your friend Sally's for a sleepover!" We speak this way as leaders, team builders, colleagues, friends, and parents. It's called, manipulation. When you tell your child to eat something, *or else*, no dessert, **you** as the parent have just placed a negative thought or intention into your child's mind. Your child suddenly begins to feel anxiety, pressure, and stress, causing them to mumble unpleasant things about you under their breath.

I want to share with you a philosophy called "Brian's Broccoli Theory." This will help you when you're faced with a difficult situation or a pessimistic personality. The whole premise of my broccoli theory is to give the **positive end result**. Here it is in action. "Hey Bobby, *when* you eat your broccoli, you *will* have dessert!" "Susie, *when* you clean your room, I'll take you to Sally's *immediately!*" As soon as you tell your children, "When you eat your broccoli, you will have dessert," guess what they start thinking about…dessert. This is the positive end result! They know if they don't eat the broccoli, they're not getting any dessert, but you don't have to *tell* them that.

The next time you're confronted with a difficult situation or a negative co-worker, try some broccoli. "Hey Fred, I know you are unhappy with all this team building stuff and would rather not participate, but let me give you a few *benefits* of being on this team. **First**, you will have more comradeship and assistance then ever before. **Secondly**, I notice that sometimes you are in the office late at night trying to complete your work. Being on the team will *help* alleviate that. It will certainly also help your permanent record and pay raise possibilities." Once you fill each person's mind with all the **positive** benefits, they most assuredly will begin to think positively.

How many times have you said this to your children, "If you don't pick up those toys, you're not going anywhere!?" Perhaps you said it right before you started to read this book. Whenever you said it, what was the last thing your child heard? "You're **not** going!" From the get go, your child already thinks he/she is not going anywhere. The tears begin to form in their eyes and the whining starts. Now, listen to Brian's Broccoli Theory. "When you pick up your toys, you can go!" The last thing your child heard you say was what? "You **can** go!" Your child begins thinking, "Mom and dad said I can go. What do I have to do again? Oh yes, pick up my toys." This theory has been proven effective many times over.

Let me share with you how I utilized this theory with a family member. Awhile back my wife and I took our four-year old niece Samantha to Pizza Hut on kids night. That was an experience in itself. We ordered a kid size personal pan pizza that came with a small toy When the pizza arrived at our booth, my niece took one bite out of one slice of pizza and then dove straight for the toy. I promptly took the toy away and pushed the pizza back in front her, stating, "Samantha, sweetie, *when* you eat your pizza, uncle "B" will *give* you this toy." Samantha noticed we were eating and suddenly perceived the message, "As soon as I eat my food, I'll get my toy!" She began gobbling down her pizza like there was no tomorrow.

Put the broccoli theory into practice, using it in every situation you may find it necessary. I guarantee you will make progress. Is it 100 percent effective all the time? Of course not, most things in life are not, but it does work. My advice is to start slowly and begin programming it into your communicator style. Next time you're dealing with negativity or uncertainty try a little "vegetable talk."

Personal pit stops and oil changes allow us to obtain a fresh perspective on life. Many times, all we need is a little "air in our tires" to get through the day. Other times, we require complete overhauls. When your car has an oil change or tune-up, how do you feel when the procedure is over? Usually, we feel safe and secure as well as happy and comfortable. The same I'VE GOT GAS concept applies again.

We need to start living life in the present. Is it bad to dream about the future? Not at all, but if all you are doing is living in the future, you may be missing some enjoyable things in the present. The past is just what it says it is, the past. The sentence you just read is in the past, the last breath you exhaled is in the past, the way you just moved your arm is in the past. These things can never be repeated. Certainly they may be duplicated, but never actually repeated, otherwise we would not have a past. Remember this quotation, "The past is history, the future is a mystery, today is a gift, that's why it's called the **present**."

We can learn from the good and bad events of our past, but should never dwell on them. Although we can be proud of ourselves for performing well, let's never forget to *continue* to do our best. If a baseball pitcher throws a perfect strike, he or she cannot rely on that one pitch, as many more strikes are required to win the game. They can learn from that pitch and make every attempt to duplicate it, but they can never win the game by dwelling on it.

We tend to look into our "rearview mirror" of life too often. While driving, it's normal for one to glance into the rearview mirror quite subconsciously. We all do it. We like to analyze what's "behind" us. The things you see in the rearview mirror are just that, behind you. If you continue to live your life looking into the rearview mirror, you might miss the beautiful scenery up ahead. You cannot change or control the past, but you can most definitely change and control your current attitude. Situations that have occurred in the past are not likely to fade from your mind, but your views and feelings about them can. You cannot change what you see behind you in the rearview mirror, but you *can* change the person staring back! Next time you look into your rearview mirror, say "Hi" to someone who loves you. Every morning you should take time to view your positive self in the mirror, realizing that you *are* the fairest of them all. Start appreciating yourself today and begin forgiving yourself for yesterday!

This fourth Mile Marker was designed to help you realize that pit stops and oil changes are not only essential to your vehicle, but also apply to your own body. Let's take much better care of ourselves in every way. Have you visited your Positive Pit-Crew lately? You are your own internal engine. It's up to you to make certain your motor is running smoothly. Become your own mechanic and give yourself a tune-up!

CRUISIN' CONCEPTS TO CONSIDER...

- *Reflect on your Positive Pit-Crew*

- *Change is good*

- *Self check-ups are great*

- *Listen to your screech strips*

- *Brian's Broccoli Theory*

HEADLIGHTS AND INTERIOR LIGHTS

"Triumph is directly proportional to the amount of 'umph'
that goes behind the try."

- Penny Pennington

Every car, whether it cost $150,000 or $2,500, requires a set of headlights. They were added to automobiles to help guide us through the darkness. What if headlights were not available and your car had to run with oodles of flashlight batteries? That would definitely place batteries as the world's "number one best seller." Headlights allow us to clearly navigate through dimly lit areas. How are your internal headlights? Are they shining brightly enough to guide you through the dismal areas of your life? This is a great moment to find out.

Several years ago I was given the fortunate opportunity to teach public speaking and interpersonal communication courses at a local university. I met many wonderful students who were fun to be around. One day, while sitting in the student center drinking a cup of coffee, Amy, one of my students, approached me and said.

"Brian, you have a spotlight for an inner light."

I was a bit confused by her statement. "What do you mean, Amy?"

"Simple," she said. "My grandmother always judges people by their inner light. Some have a bright inner illumination and a positive outlook on life, while others have a dull spark and possess a negative outlook. You have a light that sends out the strength and power of a lighthouse beacon!" Blushing, I thanked her for that compliment. Her comment actually gave me GAS. (Or was it the cafeteria food? No, it was the comment.)

Since that day, Amy's message has stayed with me. When I meet new individuals, I am constantly searching for their inner light. When I notice they have a dull inner-bulb, I try to give them a "jumpstart." It could be something as simple as a compliment or smile. Everyone deserves an opportunity to have an efficient system. Thanks, Amy, and thank you Amy's grandmother for your inner light theory.

I truly believe *good* people are born into this world. Traveling along the road of life we will experience many joyful and tragic events. Individuals that have become distraught, may need recharged. Their inner light may at one time have radiated brightly, but now it is dull. Will you always know the reason for this if it happens? Maybe, maybe not, but ignoring it, does not make it any better. People need jumpstarted every once in a while just like their cars do. The phrase, "Leave home at home and work at work," is easier said then done. If someone is going through a divorce, their anxiety will most assuredly follow them to work, whether they want it to or not. If you are running into financial difficulties at home or experiencing problems with your children, they are coming to work with you also. If you have a bad day at the office because your boss is a "goof," some of that frustration is definitely accompanying you back home. That's life.

I do agree we have to watch bringing mental thoughts in "excess" to work or home, but it is almost impossible not to have at least *some* emotions follow us. Try using diplomacy with others and view the good they have to offer. The next time you encounter an individual whose lights are dim, don't be so quick to judge, but instead, be quicker to jumpstart!

I am certain you will agree that, "Some folks is jest plain ole' ornery," to quote an old cowboy point of view. There are a large percentage of people who have their inner light shining at different wattage for various reasons that only they can explain. Tell people that you admire their bright inner light when you see it. Help others jumpstart their dim inner light when they need it.

How many times have you had a dead car battery and needed someone to help you with jumper cables? Most everyone has had this happen at least once. When you found that kind, patient person who lent you a helping hand by jumpstarting your battery, how did you feel? Take the time to recharge a friend or possibly a complete stranger requiring assistance. Share your positive energy with others. If you have enough "juice" within yourself, why not spread the wealth.

We need to remember to give *ourselves* a jumpstart every once in a while. Sometimes we require a kick in the rear in order to put ourselves back in gear. I'll admit, there are days when I need a generator to help brighten my inner light. On those days when I'm feeling completely depleted of energy, I head straight to my "jumper cable" file. What is a jumper cable file you may ask? It is a file containing positive feedback. When I became a professional speaker, I began a file consisting of letters, e-mail, cards, and notes that past participants in my seminars have written to me. When I am in need of a boost, I turn to that file for encouragement. It is easy to forget that we <u>all</u> have the power to influence others in a most positive way. That file is a reminder of why I have chosen my career. Reading memos and correspondence from old friends, as well as strangers, gives me the GAS and jumpstart I need to feel revved up and rejuvenated.

Do you have some sort of jumper cable file? I'm sure in the past you have kept a note from someone special or hung a certificate of recognition on your wall. Why? Probably for the same reason I did, self-reminders. If you have no jumper cable memories, start creating them. You can keep a file of all of the good things *you* have done for others. It is your own personal jumper cable file for the sole purpose of feeling good about yourself. I do not even share this file with my family. It is mine alone. When was the last time you took the time to sort through your file? Try it today. Remember it's for you and you alone.

All cars are equipped with low and high beams. Have you ever thought of yourself as having low and high beams? It is important to see clearly while cruisin' the road of life. We all get involved in situations where we see no light at the end of the tunnel. It is during these times we must switch on our high beams and view the BIG picture. It's hard to see the big picture when you're standing inside the frame. Learn to step *outside* the frame every once in a while and examine your life from another angle. Let your light shine. You may be surprised at what you see.

Let's discuss the game, "highway follow-the-leader." I know you have participated at least once while driving. The game is played as follows: One car (a complete stranger to you, who usually has a fuzz buster) takes the leadership role while other cars decide to follow. If the lead car switches lanes, everyone switches lanes. If it speeds up, everyone speeds up. If it slows down, everyone slows down. It's much like the analogy I mentioned in Mile Marker #1 about setting the pace. When this follow-the-leader game is being played, it's as though you have latched onto a weird connection with the other cars involved. The longest game I have ever played lasted 95 miles. There were three cars involved, two others and my own. I was positioned in the middle, which is the safest place to be during the game. (If you do happen to pass a state trooper, chances are the last car will be the one pulled over.)

We were moving out and making great time. The lead car, occupied by one male, was doing everything right. When he was obliged to pass a slower car, he did so and we followed. When it was necessary that he slow down, he did and we followed. It was as though we were one big happy family. When it finally came time for the lead car to exit the highway, he actually turned around and waved to me and the third player. It was as though he were saying, "Hi, and thanks for playing the game. It was fun!" Strangely, it provided amusement to the participants. So, a few miles down the road, when it was my turn to exit, I also turned and waved to the minivan behind me. The whole family of four smiled and waved back! It was a great inner feeling. The moral of the story: *Will you be able to lead others when it is your turn?* Being called upon to lead may happen at any moment. Is your inner light shining brightly enough for others to follow? Can your inner light guide you and others on your journeys through life?

Most racing fans would agree that races are won or lost in the turns. Anyone can follow a rapid pace in a straight line. When life is dealing you aces, you are on top of the world. You become a little bit friendlier, a lot more patient and you smile at everyone. The true test is what kind of driver are you when it comes to the "turns?" Life is full of twists and turns. For instance, when your boss criticizes you or when you wreck your car. These are defining moments when you switch on the high beams and look within yourself. Do you need some "corner work" so to speak? See what your heart has to say about the situation and act accordingly. Be proud of your maneuvering ability.

One of the many organizations that demonstrates the art of customer service, quality, and the inner light theory is the Saturn Corporation. When they say, "A different kind of car, a different kind of company," they're not joking. This company is well known for their service. A few years back my mother-in-law (the fifth grade teacher) bought a Saturn. The men and women at our local dealership took on the role of friend instead of pushy salesperson. Saturn's "No Hassle, No Haggle" sales policy is just what they say it is. Since purchasing her new car she has had nothing but positive things to say about the experience. If a car company such as Saturn can have a "No Hassle, No Haggle" policy, then why can't we adopt the same philosophy? When was the last time, without hassle or haggle, you let your inner light shine?

Have you ever flashed your high beams or flicked your headlights on and off to inform approaching motorists of the state highway patrol car you just passed? I have signaled other drivers in this manner several times. Why do we do it? Perhaps to create a bond between unsuspecting driver's whom you'll never meet, but want to help nevertheless. In a way, you have become "connected" with those individuals who would have received a rather expensive speeding citation had it not been for your preventative high beam intervention. I get good vibrations when someone does this for me. It's nice to know that someone made an effort to save my hide.

While you continue to cruise through life, keep in mind the caution power you possess. Some people, for whatever reason, have become blind to obstacles waiting up ahead. Showing a genuine concern for another's well being, is a tremendous way to share your GAS. When was the last time you flashed your "personal" headlights in the direction of a friend or stranger?

Applying these methods to *yourself* is a good idea. Special BULLETIN... You are your own best friend. I sure hope you like yourself! You can fool others but you cannot fool yourself. You can close your eyes and imagine perfection, but the moment you open them, reality kicks in. Your age, your color, your receding hairline, your weight, your attitude, and your integrity are just that, yours. Accept yourself for who you are today and remember, the only one stopping you from becoming that person you would like to be tomorrow, is you! The Serenity Prayer says it best. "God grant me the Serenity to accept the things I cannot change, Courage to change the things I can, and Wisdom to know the difference."

When a brand new car rolls off the assembly line it's shiny, appealing, and in top working condition. No matter what make or model. However, after a period time, things begin to "wear out." The tires may have had tread when they left the dealership, but as the miles go by, a rotation or change may be necessary. How much does this sound like the human body? The majority of our interior and exterior accessories need to be maintained in order to function properly.

To date, I have owned six cars. Some were nice and some were hunks of junk that should not have been allowed on the road. My "junkers" became worse in appearance because of my attitude towards them. You could look into the back seat and see exactly where I ate dinner that week. There were fast food wrappers on the seat and floor, bags from anywhere and junk from everywhere. It was disgusting! I chose to make the interior nothing less than a garbage bin. My attitude was that I drove nothing more than a clunker, so what did I care? It was like the self-fulfilling prophecy.

Then I began dating. When I realized my date would have to sit on a mountain of "happy meals," I decided to clean my car inside and out. Every time I performed that labor, including polishing, waxing, and vacuuming every inch of the car, I felt good about myself. There is nothing more pleasant than traveling in a clean and fresh smelling car. It puts you in a better state of mind. Our "spirits" require this clean-up as well.

If you are not happy with your personal interior, give yourself a "clean sweep." Get rid of anything that may pollute or clutter your interior, be it fast food wrappers of dishonesty, gossip, hatred, or untruths. It doesn't matter, as these things are only temporary. Throw out negativity, then pick your cleansed and polished self up and begin again. Believe me, you'll be glad you did and your interior will feel much better. Start cleaning clutter when you first notice it beginning to form. It's much easier this way.

Automotive interior lights are a helpful nighttime feature. When the door is opened, these strategically located illuminating sources provide enough power to assist you while getting in and out. They help you find that something in your purse, or allow you to find the keys you dropped on the floor. No matter for what reason they are used, they assist both the driver and passengers in many ways. Are *your* interior lights turning on when you need them?

What's on the inside is far more important than our outside appearance. Society, however, has upset this concept by placing emphasis on *how* we look, rather then *who* we are. When was the last time you read a magazine designed solely for the purpose of "interior" beauty? Why do clothing magazines require models robed in threads of splendor? Why can't they simply display the clothing without a model? We know the answer to that, don't we? Beauty sells. Makeup, hair products, teeth whiteners, implants, electrolysis, fake nails, cosmetic surgery, and exotic underwear, were created with the sole purpose of making our exteriors look like a million dollars. Just remember, in an instant it could all change. A zit, blemish, or bad hair day can appear at the drop of a dime. Centering your life around the exterior, and not focusing enough on the interior, is harmful. The interior of your soul is a special place. We need to be proud of ourselves, not just when we reach high peaks and feel great, but also during bumpy and rough times. Stop and think of one good thing you did today utilizing your interior light system. How did it feel? Did it give you GAS? Don't let your interior light become dim! Do you see others for their exterior or interior?

If you have ever owned or ridden in a convertible, then you already know what a thrill they can be. There's nothing quite like cruisin' with the top down on a balmy summer day. It's just you, the wind, and the open road. A convertible's interior is exposed to everyone. Wouldn't it be true to say then, that our personal interiors could be just as exposable? Opening up to others can be a wonderful experience. Put your "top down" whenever you feel the need for some fresh air!

Did you ever stop to think for a moment how much we talk to our cars? We converse with them as if they can somehow hear what we are saying. Sometimes we pat the dash, begging our car to make it the nearest gas station. And other times we're complaining to it about the strange noises it's making. Our vehicles are our friends and they need tender loving care. Most positive "car talk" occurs when we are washing it. We say, "Oh, baby. You really shine today!" or "Mommy/daddy is proud of you." Some go as far as to kiss the car after cleaning. Isn't it true we as human beings require the same love and attention? When was the last time you talked positive to yourself and were proud of your accomplishments? You are your own internal engine and you will only look and feel as good as you treat yourself.

A useful feature that all cars come equipped with is the glove compartment or box. This is the small-concealed compartment on the passenger's side of the car in which we store "stuff." I don't know why we call it a "glove" compartment? I mean who actually keeps gloves inside? No matter, the fact remains that this space is there for us to use as we wish. Here's what I keep in mine: car registration, title, maintenance manual, jumper cable notes from my wife, pictures, toll tickets, gum, sales receipts, small notes or numbers that I don't want to lose but I'm not sure why I'm keeping them, sunglasses, and finally, a spare key to my house. What do you keep in yours? Why do you keep it there? Simple, it would clutter up your interior if it were not hidden. We put stuff into the glove box because it is *easily* accessible and we know exactly where it is at all times. Now, ask yourself, what do you keep in your *internal* glove compartment? Are you keeping happy memories or sad memories? Are you keeping positive thoughts or storing negative grudges? Is your glove compartment full or do you still have room?

The internal glove box is the perfect place for you to store **happy, fun** memories and **positive** thoughts. Keep your internal glove box accessible. It can be visited and opened at anytime. Put <u>good</u> and <u>necessary</u> things inside and leave out the "stuff" that makes you upset or negative. Next time you're feeling dull, open your glove box and pull out a positive memory.

The trunk of your car is another source of storage. It holds the spare tire and jack, jumper cables, flares, possibly a few blankets, or maybe even a shovel for when we get stuck in the snow. The trunk storage space however, is *not* as accessible as the glove compartment. The glove box can be easily opened by the driver or passenger at anytime. Whereas one needs to *stop* the vehicle and walk around to the rear in order to gain entrance into the trunk. What are you keeping in your *internal* trunk? If you are going to hold on to **bad** memories or **negative** emotions (and I hope you don't) keep them in your trunk instead of your glove box. If they are kept in the larger trunk area, some *serious* thinking is required to get them out. Visit your happy glove compartment memories anytime and try to refrain from digging in the trunk too often.

Let me share with you one of my mother's favorite, happy, glove box memories about her little boy, me. The setting takes place in kindergarten when I was only six years old. One day I came home from school very excited. I explained to my mom that my excitement came from knowing everyone in my class liked me.

"How do you know this?" She asked.

With a smile on my face I replied, "In class today I asked all the other boys and girls to raise their hands if they liked me."

"That's great. Did everyone raise their hands?"

"No, but some of the kids must not have heard me ask the question!" Talk about the power of positive thinking. I definitely had it that day.

Here's a somewhat **funny** memory from my mom's glove box. This memory could have become trunk storage, but because she laughs about it today, it fits neatly into her glove compartment.

When I was two years old I used to bite and kick people for no apparent reason. If we were holding hands in prayer around the dinner table, I would reach over and bite my brother's hand. Why did I do such a thing? Since I was definitely not related to any saber tooth tigers where I would have possibly inherited biting as a characteristic trait, I suppose being in the "terrible two" phase of my life was the only possible excuse.

It became so bad that I began biting complete strangers.

One day she was entertaining a friend who came to our home for a visit. They were sitting in the kitchen having lunch when I strolled in.

"What a sweet little boy," the friend said. At that precise moment I kicked her in the shin and ran away. She yelled in pain. My mother was not only embarrassed, but definitely angry. This was big time trouble for my little self. Coal was a popular gift *that* Christmas. Her memory of my "kicking" escapade is glove box material because of the humor it brings her today.

Remember my friend Tom? My internal glove box is filled with pleasant memories of our relationship. However, the tragic events and circumstances of his untimely death, are stored in my trunk.

Let's discuss lane changing for a moment. In driver education class we studied when and when not to change lanes. We learned about the single yellow line, the double yellow line, and the dashed yellow line. Nowadays, most of us ignore the rules of passing. Not much attention is being paid to the yellow lines on the road. Once, I witnessed a car passing another car by driving over the cement, one-foot barrier that runs down the center of the road. Certainly anyone who drives over cement dividers knows this is considered a driving danger. This move is not legal in any state. It is also unlawful and dangerous to pass on a winding road or up a hill. Why so many people take such unnecessary risks is beyond me. Yellow lines are painted on the roadways for a reason, to give you guidance.

Life is full of hills and bends. If you decide to bear down on the gas pedal of life, just be certain to use caution and only pass on the yellow dashed lines. Are you following your "yellow lines" in life or have you strayed from the path?

The brochure *Responsible Driver,* put out by the Ohio Department of Public Safety, has some additional passing traffic tips. There are some things so basic to traffic safety that many drivers tend to forget altogether how to practice good driving habits. Thousands of accidents are caused every year by failure to yield and not paying attention. Knowing how and when to pass is critical to being a competent skilled driver. It is important to use your turn signal when passing other vehicles and changing lanes. Using your signal allows other drivers to know you plan to pass or make a lane change. Once you make a lane change, be certain your turn signal a.k.a. "blinker" is turned off.

Blinkers allow others to know your intentions. Do you use your *internal* blinkers the same way? Make sure the messages you are sending others are the *same* messages they are receiving. When you use your left turn signal and the person behind you perceives that signal to mean your turning left, once you make the turn communication occurs. What's scary is that interpersonal communication may not always be as clear as our blinkers.

For many years, communication scholars have been debating the issue of the term "communication." There are many definitions. We'll focus on two of the most common. **Definition #1:** "One cannot, *not* communicate. Everything *is* communication." According to this belief, the way you dress, the style of your eye-glasses, the carpet pattern in your home, or perhaps the way your cup sits on a table, are all communication. **Definition #2:** "Everything is *not* communication." A message must be **intentionally** sent *and* **intentionally** received in accordance with the manner in which the sender intended. If that happens, then communication occurred. A mutual understanding on <u>both</u> sides makes it communication. Which definition is correct? We may never know the answer.

I believe the *second* definition to be more realistic. I am not saying you're wrong if you believe the first definition, there are still highly reputable communication scholars who do. In fact, for years I believed the first definition, until I did some research, studying, and a *lot* of communicating. Here is what I found. Almost every time you interact with another human being, whether it's with your spouse, friend, child, co-worker or client, about 50 percent is communication, while the remaining balance, is perception. I am a firm believer that we *perceive*, way more than we *communicate*. We could debate all day long regarding this issue. No matter how good the debate may be, it actually boils down to semantics. I, like others, believe that in order for communication to be called communication, a mutual understanding must occur.

If the receiver interprets the intended message incorrectly, that is perception rather than communication. Confusing? Perhaps a bit, so let me give you a few examples clarifying my point. Imagine yourself discussing "apples" with someone, only to discover that throughout the entire conversation they thought you were talking about "oranges." What would you call that? Perhaps you would call it a misunderstanding or miscommunication. But, I believe if something is <u>mis</u>communication, it cannot be communication *until* the "intended" message is understood.

What would you think if I cross my arms while speaking to you? Perhaps words like defensive, arrogant, bored, angry, or aggravated might come to mind. What if I were <u>just</u> comfortable? If I did it for comfort and you thought I did it for *that* reason, communication would have occurred. If however, you believed I was *not* comfortable and instead were thinking those other thoughts, I would say you were perceiving my behavior to be whatever it was *you* wanted it to be. I would not call the process communication, but rather, perception of behavior because you see, I did cross my arms <u>only</u> to be comfortable.

I used the following example at the university while teaching a course on interpersonal communication. Every semester I would debate the two general definitions. The debate usually lasted all semester. Half the class would agree with me while the other half thought I was insane.

One day, I decided to do something different to convince them of my way of thinking.

I wore a navy blue suit to class with one bright yellow sock and one navy blue sock. However, I never mentioned the socks during the entire class period, but my movements made both colors visible. I sat on the desk and folded my legs exposing both socks as if nothing were wrong. Just before class was over I asked the students, "Who noticed my yellow sock today?" Instantly, all the hands went into the air. I pointed to one student and asked, "John, what are my mismatched socks communicating to you? What is the communication process here?" "You're a weirdo!" He replied. I couldn't have agreed more. I then pointed to another student and asked the same question. This student thought I was communicating my need for fashion tips. I pointed to another student and asked the question one final time. "What are my mismatched socks communicating to you?" This student actually said, "You're a cool, hip dude!" I did not realize that one yellow sock with a navy blue suit would classify me as a cool, hip dude, but the fact remained. I communicated with one student that I was a weirdo. I communicated with another student that I was a tacky dresser. I had a communication process with yet another student that I was a cool, hip dude. I then said to the class, "Wouldn't it be funny if I were to tell you that your instructor is color blind!" A hush fell over the classroom. "I had no intention of putting on a yellow sock this morning, therefore I had <u>no</u> intention of communicating anything!" However, all three students **perceived** something different.

The moral of the story is that I did not intend to communicate at all that day (except to make a point), but the class perceived many things. Thus my belief that everything is NOT necessarily communication but rather a perception of behavior or a perception in one's own mind. What are the signs and signals you are sending to others? Are your "signals" being interpreted correctly?

This fifth Mile Marker was designed to allow you to reflect on your own interior light. Is yours shining brightly enough? Are you in need of a jumpstart? Have you stored glove box memories and do you visit them often? Are the messages you send to others the same as those they receive?

CRUISIN' CONCEPTS TO CONSIDER...

- *Jumpstart your inner light*

- *Take the lead when your chance arrives*

- *Accentuate your interior*

- *Visit your glove box and jumper cable file often*

- *Make sure your internal blinkers work properly*

Here's a note for your jumper cable file

Dear Friend,

   You are wonderful. I hope you have a fantastic day ☺ Keep your smile alive and if you see someone without one, give them one of yours. Make the most out of today and never forget, you are someone special!

                    Your pal,
                    Brian Blasko

P.S. I'VE GOT GAS

ROAD MAPS AND DESTINATIONS

"A journey of a thousand miles begins with one step"

- Lao-Tzu

When you get into your vehicle, you generally have a destination in mind. Maybe it's the local ice cream shop or your favorite bookstore. You paint a mental image of where you intend to go. As we continue our journey through life, the same philosophy applies. Do you know *your* destinations? Do you have a vision for the future? If we cruise through life with no direction, then our outcomes are unpredictable. Keep in mind, having direction does not always mean you will not or cannot get lost along the way. It was Will Rogers who said it best, "Even if you're on the right track, you'll still get run over if you just stand there."

When we achieve our goals we feel success and fulfillment. Some may define success as winning a triathlon, writing a book, making a million dollars, or knitting a sweater. Be specific with your dreams and be ready to work for anything you truly want from life. Nothing comes easy. This Mile Marker was created to allow time to ponder the age old question, why am I here, what is my purpose?

Growing older is an ongoing process that only ends when your number is called. In fact, your age is the only thing that will always go up but never come down. In grade school, we all had dreams and visions about what we wanted to do when we grew up. Believe it or not, I know some *adults* who still have no clue what they want to be when they grow up! Are you today, what you had wished to become yesterday? If the answer is no, what's stopping you?

When I was in second grade, I was a "van" child. This meant going to a large recreational vehicle outside of the school building, where students who were struggling received additional help. My problem was speech. Can you believe it? A public speaker, actually had trouble speaking a youngster. I was unable to enunciate certain words clearly. For example, instead of saying *grill*, I would say *girl*. It was actually funny when I asked if we could cook out on the girl. I wasn't concerned with the benefits of proper speech. My goal was to be normal like all of the other kids. What actually *is* normal? At the time, I thought normal meant anyone who didn't have to attend classes in the van. It did not matter if I spoke improperly. What did matter was that I become like the regular kids who stayed in school for all of their classes. My fixation with this "normalcy" was causing me to feel inadequate.

I was released from the van after one full year. I am happy to report that I can enunciate "grill" (and many other words) properly. I was successful in achieving my goal of rejoining the normal kids for all of my classes. To this day I am still proud of the improvement I made in my speech.

Society influences our emotions. In *my* mind, "society" was saying that normal kids stayed inside the school building to be taught. Therefore, having to go to the van caused me to feel abnormal. Why do we let society set the rules for us? My advice is to take the driver's seat and let the dictates of society ride shotgun for awhile.

The fourth grade was by far my most disastrous year in school. Miss "D" and I never saw eye-to-eye on anything. It seemed I managed to even raise my hand wrong half the time. I suppose some of the conflict arose from the fact that I tried harder than anyone to be the class clown. I spent most of that year either in the corner or in the principal's office. I visited the principal so many times I actually had a seat with my name on it.

One day, three other students and I finally pushed Miss "D" over the edge. She gave the four of us a permanent corner for the rest of the year and told the class we were invisible and that we were not to be looked at or spoken to. This new seating arrangement continued for weeks and I began to feel depressed. I felt unimportant and starved for attention. Something had to change soon. One day Miss "D" was teaching a lesson on creativity. She explained that successful people are creative and have vivid or wild imaginations. I thought this description fit me perfectly. However, I was not feeling very creative while sitting in the corner.

I developed a plan that I was absolutely certain Miss "D" would find imaginative and creative. My idea would make her realize such a creative genius, should <u>not</u> be in the corner. On our lunch break, I convinced the "corner boy gang" to follow my lead. As soon as the afternoon lesson began, I gave the secret signal and my buddies and I got up out of our seats and began walking around the classroom. We were up for about 20 seconds when we heard a monstrous scream from the front of the room. "What are you boys doing?!" Here was my moment to shine and prove to Miss "D" and the class that I was a creative person. I very calmly and casually said, "We're invisible, remember? You and the class cannot see us so please continue with your lesson." The class immediately erupted with laughter and I felt great inside. I was back!

Miss "D," however, did not see the humor or creativity in my little stunt. Once again I found myself making that ever too familiar journey towards the principal's office to sit in my "favorite chair." Perhaps pretending to be invisible was not the correct thing to do. But I did let creativity reign! There is a bit of Miss "D" in each of us that every once in a while stifles our own creativity. Next time you hear that shrieking voice, stick it in the trunk.

Your dreams, visions, and goals are only as real as you think they are. Having the right road map definitely helps. The D-R-I-V-E-R technique, a successful goal setting strategy, is the road map I use.

DRIVER

D — E T A I L E D

R — E A L I S T I C

I — N I T I A T E — A C T I O N O U T L I N E

V — E R I F Y — T I M E S

E — N T H U S I A S M

R — E C O R D

Detailed: Be specific about what you want. *I want to lose 20 pounds by May 1, so I can fit into my new outfit that I plan to wear for an upcoming party. I've had my eye on someone special who will be there and I'd like to look and feel good about myself. Losing weight will give me the confidence I need for this occasion.* This is detailed and specifies my goal. *I want to quit smoking because I am spending entirely too much money on this habit. I am tired of being the "outcast" and having people tell me my clothes stink and that my breath is bad. I also want to live longer.* That is **detailed**. If you want to buy a new car be specific. Merely stating that you want to purchase a new automobile is too vague. State *exactly* what your preference is by thinking it through. *I want a new, silver, automatic, four door sedan, spoiler on the trunk, CD player, with a sun roof, for under $18,000.* When you make the goal that **detailed,** it is much easier to go shopping for your dream car. The more detailed your personal goals are, the easier it is to envision the finish line.

Realistic: Be aware of setting unrealistic goals. Think your goals through thoroughly. When we do not achieve our goals, it could be because the expectations being set are unrealistic. To say you want to become a millionaire by tomorrow is an unrealistic goal. Could it happen? Certainly, if you hit the lottery, but the odds are against it. Think about your goal with **realism** and then proceed accordingly. Before I began writing this book, I had to determine if I had the talent to convey my message in a readable and interesting way. Did I have the time to write it? Did I have the means to publish it? Could I find an editor? Would anybody buy it? These were just a few of the **realistic** questions I had to ponder. Once you've decided your goal is realistic, step on the gas!

Initiate action outline: In this stage baby steps begin. For example, if your goal is to lose weight, you can't expect the pounds to just "melt" away. You need a plan of action.

Action outline

Week One:	Observe and log present eating habits and walk 15 minutes daily.
Week Two:	Eliminate all "junk food" and walk 30 minutes daily.
Week Three:	Drink 5 glasses of water a day and do 20 sit-ups daily.
Week Four:	Cut your meal portions in half and do 35 sit-ups daily.
Week Five:	Observe progress, alter the plan where necessary and continue on.
Week Six:	Increase exercise reps and shop for an outfit in your "new" size.

The **action outline** allows you to measure your progress. While writing this book I used an action outline. Month One: I researched motivational books. Month Two: I created chapter themes. Month Three: I wrote down personal stories and quotes for each chapter. Month Four: I picked my editor and publisher. Month Five: I began Mile Marker #1. Month Six: I began Mile Marker #2. Month Seven: I took my first two Mile Markers to my editor. Month Eight: I began Mile Marker #3, etc. My **action outline** allowed me to make certain I was still on task. Action outlines need to be reevaluated and adjusted now and then. Following an action outline requires self-discipline. Stay the course!

Verify times: Set time limits for your goal. Start dates, sub-step dates, and end dates are required. **Start dates** are most important, but the easiest to forget. We have all been guilty of saying something like *I want to lose 10 pounds by May 1*. That's fine, but remember, you will also need to say that on April 1 you will start the weight loss process. **Sub-step dates** make up your action outline. These are the baby steps that need to occur before the goal can be achieved. **End dates** complete the time frame for your goal. If you do not accomplish your goal by the end date you have chosen, it does not mean you have failed. You need to stop and evaluate the situation. What was the reason for not completing your goal? Maybe your action outline was a bit off-schedule, or perhaps some important details were lacking. There is always a reason. A simple case of *laziness* may be your roadblock. If you are behind, step on the gas, reset your end date, and don't give up!

Enthusiasm: In this stage of the goal setting process, self mo-tivation must come alive. If you lack enthusiasm and energy for your goals, it may be more difficult to accomplish them. At times, your inspi-ration may be tough to maintain. Keeping your eye on the desired outcome and practicing positive "self-talk" is encouraging. If you are working on a team goal your **enthusiasm**, will spread to others. The same concept applies to personal goals. The more **excited** you are about your own goals, the easier it is to cross the finish line.

Record: The final stage of the DRIVER technique is simply to **WRITE IT DOWN**. The mind is a powerful thing and can retain much information. At the same time, much information can escape. Recording your goals is absolutely vital to the process. Do you need to purchase an expensive leather bound journal to record your goals? Of course not. I keep a 59 cent journal with $100,000 goals inside.

Many people say they do not have time or it isn't necessary to write everything down. WRONG. We write down things almost everyday merely to assist our memory bank. For example, have you ever been grocery shopping? Have you ever made a list? Why did you make that list? The number one reason is, "I'll forget something at the store if it is not written down." The number two reason, "I'll end up buying more than I need if I do not make a list." If you're going to spend the time and energy to write down butter, milk, and cheese, then why not spend time writing down your goals and dreams? Keep your goals and dreams **recorded** where you can revisit them frequently.

Take a moment to write down five achievement goals you wish to reach. Before you begin, follow the DRIVER goal setting strategy. If you can not apply each step of the strategy, then my advice is, do not record the goal. If your goal cannot travel through the DRIVER routine, then chances are it may not be attainable, and you may have to shift gears. Record your goals *only* after thinking them through. The DRIVER technique has helped many and I sincerely hope by using it, all your dreams and goals come true.

LIST FIVE GOALS THAT YOU WANT TO ACHIEVE

1)_____

2)_____

3)_____

4)_____

5)_____

Decide which goal is the most important to achieve first and why? How can you choose which is most important? Remember when I mentioned taking the driver's seat? NOW is the time to do it! You need to decide what is important to you and your personal development. Whether your goals are professional or personal, they should be prioritized. Do what's best for you. When you determine what you personally want to achieve first, set your cruise control on a reasonable speed and GO GET THAT GOAL. After you have accomplished your first goal, pat yourself on the back, set your cruise control again and start driving towards the second goal. Focus on only one goal at a time, giving it your full attention and effort. The *average* adult has an attention span of seven to eight seconds. According to this, I lost <u>half</u> my readers after the first sentence of this book. However, all of you are *above* average, so you are excluded.

Have you ever driven somewhere, arrived safely, and then said to yourself, "How in the world did I get here?" You arrived at your destination but could not remember whether you stopped at any stoplights or flew through any stop signs. If you ever had this happen then you have experienced what I call DDD or day dream driving. Scary isn't it? This kind of driving usually occurs when we have a lot on our minds. I experience DDD about once a month while driving. How many times a month are you experiencing it in your *personal* life? Are you losing focus of your destinations and goals? When we lose focus of our personal goals, we could get stuck on the side of the road. When we try to concentrate on numerous things at the same time, something could be overlooked. While you are busy working on one thing, your mind subsequently is DDD about the other two. For example, if you are working on three separate projects consecutively, it is impossible to render 100 percent of your focus on more than one. Arrange your priorities and do not lose focus on what is *most* important to you. While on your journey through life, be aware of the DDD factor.

Believe in Yourself

Believe in yourself—in the power you have to control your own life, day by day, Believe in the strength that you have deep inside, and your faith will help show you the way. Believe in tomorrow and what it will bring—let hopeful heart carry you through, For things will work out if you trust and believe there's no limit to what you can do.

- Emily Matthews

Everyone is responsible for his or her own destinations. Sure, others may influence you, but you always have the final say. Continue to focus on YOUR destinations and be aware that others have their own which may differ from yours. While in a relationship, it is important to know what destinations your partner has mapped out. Are you plutonic friends or more? Do you both want to raise a family? Do you prefer to live in an apartment or house? Do you know each other's goals and dreams? Are they similar or different? Knowing the answers to such questions is important. If you are heading in one direction while your partner is driving in another, it will create some frustration and confusion. Is one direction better then another? Not necessarily. Make each other aware of what your checkered flag destinations are. Although you may not be in harmony with someone else's goals or dreams, do not pass judgement until you have driven a mile in their car.

At times, there are obstacles beyond our control that stand between us, and our destinations. We should not question *why* they are there, but instead, ask ourselves, *how* can we get around them? A friend sent me this great story, titled: *The Obstacle in Our Path.* In ancient times, a king had a boulder placed on a roadway. Then he hid himself and watched to see if anyone would remove the huge rock. Some of the king's wealthiest merchants and courtiers came by and simply walked around it. Many loudly blamed the king for not keeping the roads clear, but no one did anything about getting the stone out of the way. Then a peasant came along carrying a load of vegetables. Upon approaching the boulder, the peasant laid down his burden and tried to move the stone to the side of the road. After much pushing and straining, he finally succeeded. After the peasant picked up his load of vegetables, he noticed a purse lying in the road where the boulder had been. The purse contained many gold coins and a note from the king indicating that the gold was for the person who removed the boulder from the roadway. The peasant learned what many of us never understand. *Every* obstacle presents an opportunity to improve our condition. Do not let life's boulders block the pathways toward *your* destinations.

Driving on the road requires both defensive and offensive navigation. Offensive driving means you're looking out for your *own* destinations. According to a previously mentioned brochure, *Responsible Driver*, defensive driving is driving to prevent collisions from occurring in spite of the actions of others or the presence of adverse driving conditions. Both offensive *and* defensive driving are critical for a successful journey. Some days you are the bug, some days you are the windshield! Life is full of bends and curves. Keep both hands on the wheel and be aware of your surroundings. Observe the choices you are making and the circumstances that inhibit you. Eventually, the bends will straighten and the curves will soften.

If you have ever taken a cross-country journey then you know the importance of a map. Road maps were created to guide us to our destinations. It is quite simple. Follow the road map and you will arrive where you had intended. Do not follow the road map and you'll get lost. As a motivational speaker, I have the opportunity to travel frequently. Most of my speaking engagements are out of town, therefore, I must rent a car. The first thing I do when I rent a car is search for a local area map. I use it to enable me to arrive at my destination within a reasonable time. There is vast information printed on that zig-zaggy, squared-off piece of paper that few can actually fold back into its original form. This system rarely fails, but on occasion the map is very confusing and it becomes necessary for me to stop and ask for directions (setting aside my "male" ego).

I know many people who get lost all the time and because they are suffering from embarrassment, refuse to seek helpful directions and continue driving in circles. Help is around every corner since one of the job requirements of a gas station attendant is having a master's degree in "geography." In your personal life, do you seek help and ask for the assistance *you* need?

About three years ago my wife and I decided to take a hike through a large wooded area in a local park. The day was beautiful and the sun was shining brightly. We entered the woods at 4 p.m. and observed many wonderful sights. The trees were tall and the flowers were in full bloom.

While hiking through the immense forest we lost track of time and everything closed in on us as darkness descended. We knew it was time to leave. There was one problem. We were lost! It was 6:15 p.m. by the time our trail led us to a neighborhood surrounding the eastern side of the woods. Our car, however, was parked somewhere on the western side. Instead of knocking on a door and asking someone for directions, we decided to just "wing" it. Wrong move. We ventured back into the dark and ominous wooded area and made every attempt to head west. After about 45 minutes of aimless wandering, we came upon a clearing we were certain would lead us to our car, only to discover, we were back in the same neighborhood!

Now we began to worry. Once again we were presented with an opportunity to swallow our pride and seek direction. And once again, we didn't. Instead, we walked on, and on, and on, and on, and on, until we found our way out of the unknown area to a grocery store that was **three miles** away from our car! Weary and defeated, we knew it was time to finally end our "one" hour hike. We called my mother-in-law to rescue us. I don't remember seeing anyone laugh quite so hard.

My wife and I learned a valuable lesson that day. Buy a compass. More importantly, we learned that if you are lost, asking for directions is your safest bet. When was the last time you checked your *internal* compass? If for some reason you have gotten off course, never be too proud to request assistance. Your Positive Pit-Crew is standing by.

Mapping your life's destinations is an ongoing process. Many people become so consumed with their future that they forget to live in the present. Do not forget that *today* must first be lived before tomorrow ever comes. Our futures, no matter how much we plan for them, are still a mystery. Friends will come and go, relationships will blossom and wilt, jobs will be there one day and gone the next. Even if you are the world's best driver, have the nicest car and the perfect road conditions, without clear directions you may still become lost. Begin following your personal road maps. If you don't have any, create some!

This sixth Mile Marker was designed as a guide to help you achieve your life's destinations. What lies ahead is uncertain. What *is* certain, is that you are here today. Enjoy life to its fullest. Have you studied your map lately? Do you still have destinations to reach? Is your life passing before your eyes the way you imagined it?

CRUISIN' CONCEPTS TO CONSIDER...

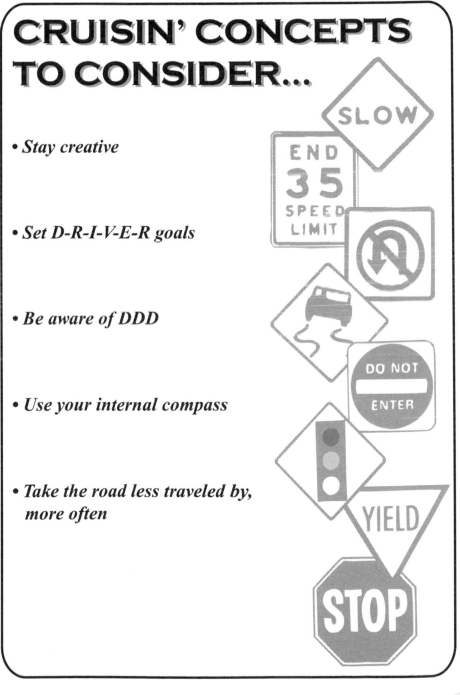

- *Stay creative*

- *Set D-R-I-V-E-R goals*

- *Be aware of DDD*

- *Use your internal compass*

- *Take the road less traveled by, more often*

Two roads diverged in

a wood, and I—

I took the one less

traveled by,

and that has made all

the difference.

-Robert Frost

May all your highways be paved with happiness. Thanks for riding shotgun with me on this journey. I wish you the best on *yours*. Now it's time to take control of the wheel and drive. Pick up your keys, start your engine, buckle your safety belt, tell yourself I'VE GOT GAS, and enjoy the ride!!!

Happy Cruisin'

ACKNOWLEDGMENTS

So many people to thank, so little time. Writing this book was an incredible journey, one I'll never forget. Through the experience, I gained valuable insight about myself and others. I received a tremendous amount of encouragement along the way from many people, and for that I am grateful.

I would like to thank Mary Lou and Steve Blasko (a.k.a. Mom and Dad) for always believing in me. Your love and support has been a blessing. You can be my driving instructors anytime.

To my beautiful wife Laura, for her continuous encouragement and love. I am fortunate to have her in my life. She is and always will be my Dollbaby. Thanks honey for always understanding and showing patience with me. You are my inspiration. I love you!

To my brothers, Steve and Dave, thanks for always looking out for your little brother. I love you both very much. Maybe one day you'll be able to beat me in a game of billiards. I also want to acknowledge my sisters-in-law, Chrissy and Lisa. Chrissy, your "illegal" driving lessons were the best and your faith in me has been great. Lisa, your thoughtfulness is refreshing and always appreciated. Thank you both for your support.

Thanks to all my friends and family. Your constant support was fabulous. A special thanks goes out to my "burning the midnight oil club." Mary Lou Blasko, Laura Blasko, Linda Susany, Lisa Susany, and the fifth grade teacher, my mother-in-law, Lisa. I appreciate all of the time and energy you gave this project. Your help will never be forgotten. You were a perfect example of a Positive Pit-Crew. Thank you so very much!

To Lisa for being such a "cool" mother-in-law and always showing faith in me as a writer, friend, and son-in-law.

Thanks to Dr. Andy Rancer and Ray Hanna for believing in me and giving me the boost I needed to "jumpstart" my career.

To Hammond's laser printing services. When I was in a bind you pulled me through.

Thanks Krissy Thurik, for the comment you made years ago that helped lead me to the title of this book.

To Rocco Seminara for all of your encouragement.

Thanks to Larry Dybis for sharing some great ideas with me. Your support and friendship is invaluable.

To Creative Literary Services and Susan, my editor, whose belief in me was top notch. Thank you for your imaginative mind and superb talent.

Many thanks to Jimmy Valentini (chairman of the board). Your artistic ability and creative juices are amazing! Thanks for all the late night hours you spent taking my vision to the next level.

Thanks to all of my clients who have brought the *Cruisin' Through Life* theme and my other workshops to your organizations. Thanks also to the many past participants who have attended my seminars and workshops. You are the reason I love my job so much.

Finally and foremost, I would like to thank the "Man" upstairs (a.k.a. **God**) for all of the gifts you have given me. I promise I will continue to use them positively.